MARY

New Century Theology

Other books in this series include:

MARY

Sarah Jane Boss

Illustrations by Neil Warmsley

New Century Theology

continuum
LONDON • NEW YORK

CONTINUUM
The Tower Building, 11 York Road, London SE1 7NX
15 East 26th Street, New York, NY 10010

www.continuumbooks.com

First published 2004

British Library Cataloguing-in-Publication Data
A catalogue record for this book is available from the British Library.

ISBN 0–8264–5788–6

Typeset by Continuum
Printed and bound in Great Britain by Cromwell Press, Wiltshire.

Contents

List of illustrations

Our Lady of Orcival (from *Histoire d'un Sanctuaire d'Auvergne, Notre-Dame d'Orcival* Société de Saint-Augustin and Desclée, de Brouwer et Cie, Lille and Paris, 1894)

Amb gràcies a la Mare de Déu de Montserrat

Preface

The question of the Virgin Mary's relationship to God's fundamental work of creation is one that has interested me for the past nineteen years or so. However, this is the first piece of specifically theological writing that I have done on the subject, and I hope it will prove to be the first stage of a long process of study that I am undertaking in the area of 'green mariology', that is, Mary's part in the theology of nature. I hope it will also encourage others to work in the same area.

In 1957, the eminent mariologist Clément Dillenschneider published a work on *Mary in the Economy of the Renewed Creation (Marie dans l'Economie de la Création Rénovée*, Paris: Editions Alsatia). His interesting monograph makes it clear that it is not just humanity, but the whole created order, that is caught up in creation's renewal, but does not suggest that there might be a connection between this theology and the conduct of our everyday lives in relation to other creatures. In the present book, I explicitly raise questions of this kind, although I do not propose answers to them.

Since the time at which Dillenschneider was writing, Mary has started to be mentioned in non-specialist books on modern science. Rupert Sheldrake, in *The Rebirth of Nature* (London: Rider, 1993), devotes a section to the Mother of God, and Theodore Roszak's *The Gendered Atom* (Dartington, Devon: Green Books, 2000) has a chapter on the black Madonna of Einsiedeln, in connection with Mary Shelley's *Frankenstein* and the particle accelerator at CERN. These authors suggest that there is some connection between discoveries in modern science, such as the mysterious nature of sub-atomic particles, or the existence of 'dark matter', and more ancient religious views. Sheldrake writes: 'This dark matter has the archetypal power of the dark, destructive Mother; it is like Kali, whose very name means "black".' This is supposed to indicate that humanity needs to abandon its confidence in a mechanistic world view, and again become more humble in relation to other creatures.

When considering this book on Mary, some readers might be inclined to think that there are similarities between the ideas put forward here and a number of modern secular theories and philosophies. I argue that Mary shares an identity with the Chaos that underlies the world at every point, even as the world emerges out of it. So this is a Marian Chaos in which all creatures participate. Rupert Sheldrake's notion of 'morphic resonance', James Lovelock's *Gaia* (Oxford University Press, 2000), or the philosophy of 'deep ecology' might all occur to one as offering points of intersection with my own suggestions. And indeed, it is no surprise if there are structural similarities between my own work and those of my older (and perhaps wiser) contemporaries who, in important respects, have similar concerns to my own. However, a key aspect of the arguments advanced here is that the world comes from, goes to, and is infused with the presence of God – that the cosmos is, like Mary, Godbearing. Since this is the truth about the world, any view of 'nature' which does not take this seriously at every turn is bound to give rise to wrong perceptions of other creatures and wrong behaviour in relation to them. Purely secular theories are therefore necessarily inadequate or mistaken when considering humanity's relationship with the natural world.

Furthermore, the view of creation that I am proposing is one that should call into question the truth and morality of the scientific procedures upon which some of the theories and practices mentioned above are based. For example, we might ask whether the use of large amounts of energy to smash particles together is a respectful way of treating our fellow creatures.

Having said that, I have to thank several scientists for sharing time, knowledge and ideas with me as I have been preparing this material. Most of the fruits of our contact will appear in other publications, but the thoughts that scientists have offered me have engaged my own throughout. Among the people who deserve special mention are Bill Adams, of the Geography Department at the University of Cambridge, and Peter Harper, of the Centre for Alternative Technology at Machynlleth (who will probably disagree with much of what I have written here, but with whom I hope to be able to pursue the discussion in the future). Jonathan Stacey read a draft of one section, and I have to thank him for his spiritual companionship during much of the preparation of this book.

On the mariological front, Rayna Ryley also read a draft of a chapter, and I thank her for her unwaveringly favourable reaction to it. The usual suspects have given me intellectual stimulation, and in particular, I thank Tina Beattie for reading a draft of a section, and Philip Endean for giving last-minute advice.

Neil Warmsley not only provided careful and delightful illustrations for this book, but also helped me to think about them.

The library staff of Queen's College, Oxford, made it possible for me to consult the rare volume containing Rámon Llull's *Liber Chaos*, and they cannot imagine the joy and satisfaction that this has given me. I hope they'll let me make a return visit.

Most of all, I have to thank Robin Baird-Smith, of Continuum International Publishing, for inviting me to write this and for making me finish it. Not that it's finished, of course.

Sarah Jane Boss
Felindre Isaf
Assumptiontide 2003

Figure 1. Annunciation with lily Crucifix, St Helen's church, Abingdon, Oxon.

1

The Lily Crucifix

In the Lady Chapel of St Helen's church in Abingdon, Oxfordshire, a sequence of paintings around the edge of the ceiling depicts a Jesse Tree. Jesse was the father of King David, the second and greatest of the kings of Israel, and from him would be descended a 'wonderful counsellor, prince of peace', according to the prophet Isaiah (9.6). This prince would be the ruler under God, on whose head would rest the favour of the Lord. For Christians, this prophecy is already fulfilled in Jesus Christ, and will come to completion at his second coming, when 'the wolf shall dwell with the lamb', 'the lion eat straw like the ox', and 'the earth shall be full of the knowledge of the Lord, as the waters cover the sea' (Isaiah 11.6–9).

The ruler foretold by Isaiah is to be 'a shoot from the stump of Jesse, and a branch [that] shall grow out of his roots'; the descendants of Jesse are accordingly represented in art as standing upon the branches of a tree. It is a common image in medieval Christian art. The first three figures, at the bottom of the tree, are Jesse, who is the root out of which it grows, then King David, and then King Solomon, David's son. Above them, there may be kings of Judah or Old Testament prophets, usually culminating in the Virgin Mary and her son Jesus Christ. According to the Gospels, Jesus was conceived by Mary miraculously, by the power of the Holy Spirit, without sexual intercourse, and Jesus' human and adoptive father, Joseph, was descended from David. But according to a long-standing tradition that ensures Jesus' physical descent from the great king, his mother Mary was also of the line of David. The Latin word for 'virgin', *virgo*, is similar to the Latin word for 'branch', *virga*, so Mary the *virgo* is the *virga* from whom Christ flowers.

The Jesse Tree in Abingdon, rather unusually, is drawn not on a vertical plan but on a horizontal one, with a vine winding around the edge of the ceiling and the sacred figures standing on its branches alongside one another. At the end of the vine we come to Joseph, the husband of the Virgin Mary, followed by an Annunciation scene, that is, a representation of the meeting between Mary and the angel Gabriel (Luke 1.26–38), by which Mary conceives her son, the Saviour of the world. In one panel there stands the angel, and two panels along, in the final image of the frieze, he is faced by the Virgin, with a dove above her representing the Holy Spirit. Between them, on the middle panel, there is a pot containing a lily with five blooms; and hanging on the lily is the figure of the crucified Christ (Figure 1).

Representations of the lily Crucifix are found only in southern Britain, and few of them now remain. This graceful painting in the church dedicated to St Helen, the woman who is attributed with having found the relic of the true cross, dates from the fourteenth century.

The lily is a common symbol in depictions of the Annunciation. It is often said to signify Mary's purity, though it may also carry connotations of fertility, both of which are relevant to the virginal conception of Christ. The five blooms recall the five wounds of Christ on the Cross, but also the five joys of Mary, which were often identified as the Annunciation, the Nativity, or birth of Christ, the Crucifixion, Christ's resurrection from the dead, and his ascension into heaven. The Crucifixion was included not only in lists of the Virgin's joys, but also in her sorrows. For the unjust execution of the Son of God was both the most terrible tragedy the world has ever known, and at the same time the greatest blessing, since, together with the subsequent resurrection, it is the action by which the world, paradoxically, is redeemed from sin and death. The figure of the dead Christ shows the horror of the cross, but the lily in bloom suggests the cross transformed into the Tree of Life.

The bringing together of Annunciation and Crucifixion is not an artistic conceit. From the moment at which Christ was conceived in his mother's womb, he was destined to die, as are all human beings. Indeed, he was conceived in order to die a particular death for the salvation of the world; and precisely because his death is the beginning of new life – in John's Gospel it is compared to the pangs of childbirth – the imagery of conception is appropriately overlaid upon that of the Crucifixion. Moreover, for many centuries it was believed that the historical date of the Crucifixion was 25th March, that is, the same date as the feast of the Annunciation. But the deepest meaning of both these events is given in the third of the anniversaries that was celebrated on that date, namely, the creation of the world. The work of redemption that begins in the Annunciation and finds its completion in the Crucifixion and risen life of Christ, is in truth a recreation of the universe, spiritual and material, from its very foundations. And Mary, who is a primary actor at the Annunciation, is present throughout God's work of creation.

The Mother of God and the Cosmos

Groundings

The town of Cardigan, at the mouth of the River Teifi in west Wales, is home to one of the most beautiful of legends about the Blessed Virgin Mary. According to a local tradition, a statue of the Virgin and Child floated down the river and was washed up on the shore at Cardigan, and in the Virgin's hand there was a lighted taper, or candle. A shrine was built to house the statue at the place where it was found, and the miraculous taper continued to burn constantly for nine years, until a man foreswore himself upon it, when it went out.[1] For several hundred years, Our Lady of the Taper was a focus of Christian pilgrimage, and St Mary's Church still stands there, marking the sacred ground.[2]

This is a story with evocative power for the Christian imagination, not least because of its central elements of water and light. The river and the taper recall the very creation of the universe – the foundations of the cosmos – described in the first three verses of the Bible (Genesis 1.1–3), the water of the river and the light of the taper calling to mind the water and light that are at the beginning of all things. The book of Genesis says that 'darkness was upon the face of the deep' as 'the spirit of God moved over the face of the waters' (1.2); and God's first act of creation is the speaking of the words, 'Let there be light' (1.3). Christians, who focus principally on the life and teachings of Jesus Christ as they are expounded in the New Testament, can sometimes lose sight of the cosmic aspects of their faith; but in fact, the Hebrew Bible's mysterious account of the world's foundation is recalled in some of the New Testament accounts of the origins of Jesus himself. The prologue to John's Gospel (John 1.1–18), for example, refers to Jesus as the Word of God, who was present with God at the beginning of all things, and who is 'the light that shines in the darkness'. Less overtly – although it has been noticed by many Christians throughout the centuries[3] – Luke's account of the Annunciation by the angel Gabriel to the Virgin Mary draws strongly on the first three verses of Genesis. Luke

1.26–38 narrates the visit of the angel to Mary of Nazareth. He tells her
that she is to be the mother of Jesus, 'the Son of the Most High', who will
inherit the throne of his ancestor King David and will rule 'without end'.
Mary accepts the word of God that is given her by the angel, and, according to the traditional reading of the text, this is the moment at which Jesus
is conceived in his mother's womb. The telling of this story seems intended to evoke the creation of the world: there are parallels between the creation and the Annunciation, which suggest that the latter is a recapitula-
tion of the former. As the earth at the dawn of the universe was 'without
form and void', so Mary is a virgin; nothing has yet been created in her. As
the spirit of God hovers over the face of the waters, so, Mary is told, the
manner of her conceiving will be that 'the Holy Spirit will come upon [her]
and the power of the Most High will overshadow [her]' (Luke 1.35). And
as God accomplishes his first act (and, indeed, subsequent acts) of creation
by means of speech, so it is by the angel's message that Mary conceives
Christ: 'Let it be to me according to your word,' she says (1.38). Jesus
Christ is himself the new creation, in whom the universe is restored and
fulfilled, and so it is only the language of God's creation of the universe
that can do justice to the cosmic significance of Christ's conception.

Mary, then, in one respect at least, stands at the Annunciation in the
same relation to God as do the waters of creation at the beginning of the
world. It is as though the world's redemption in Christ is in fact its re- creation, and that God accomplishes this re-creation by breathing and speaking afresh upon the world's foundations, in the person of Mary, whose very
flesh and blood are transformed into the divine microcosm that is her son.
Mary is the dark water, and Christ the fiery light. And this work of creation
and renewal is never-ending: indeed, if God were ever to cease this work,
then all things would fall into nothingness, since the existence of anything
at all is a continuous work of the Creator. Accordingly, the dark waters of
creation are ever present, although unseen. And in so far as the Blessed
Virgin shares an identity with the deep from before the dawn of time, she
too is mysteriously present in all things. In this and other ways, she is connected to the whole divine work of creation, as well as to the re-creation of
the world in Jesus Christ.

The principal argument of this work is that the Blessed Virgin Mary
shares an identity with the elemental matrix, or *chaos*, of which the world
is created. If we start by imagining the cosmos as fabric whose thread and
weave are ever changing, then Mary is in some sense the same as the
entire assembly of the most minute, invisible particles of the fibres of

which the world is spun and woven. She is present in all physical things as their foundation; yet at the same time, she shows the glory to which all things are called by their Creator. It is this intuition which implicitly informs much of Marian doctrine and devotion, and it also carries ethical implications for the conduct of humanity's relationship with the rest of creation. So we shall have to examine what is the nature of the elemental stuff that is symbolized by the unformed waters of Genesis. First, however, we need to consider the place of the Virgin Mary in the main body of the Christian faith.

Crossing boundaries

Each day brings us to a different aspect of this amazing land, this conjunction of the two mighty continents of the Ancient World. One day it is a bare gravel plain stretching as far as the eye can see, and then you are surprised by a small stream and thorny acacias digging deep into the sand for the little water that will help them sustain the small life that is their lot; the next day you find yourself amid stupendous ranges of solid rock, some black, some purple, some red, and you are treading the same land in which the Ancient Egyptian laboured to extract copper and turquoise – indeed, you can see the remains of his excavations still. You then come out on an open plain by the Red Sea and there you are joined by huge flocks of birds, pausing, resting for the night on the shore where you are camped, and as the sun rises, while the men perform their morning prayers, the birds rise too. They soar and wheel and call out to each other and set off in a great swooping cloud across the sea and towards their summer homes in the North. And then, opening out among cliffs more than a thousand feet in height, a wadi lies before you and life is plentiful again, with gardens of tamarisk and apple trees and fields of wheat and barley.[4]

These words are taken from the diary of a fictional character, an English lady named Anna Winterbourne. In 1901 she travels to Egypt, where she falls in love with the country and its people, and where she remains for some years after marrying an Egyptian husband. Almost a century later, a young American woman, Isabel, also goes to Egypt, where she tries to find out all she can about Anna, her great-grandmother through the female line. Isabel's name, 'Isa the fair', recalls Isis, the great goddess of the Nile, and so provides the American with another connection to the land of her mothers. These women are characters in a novel, Ahdaf Soueif's *The Map of Love*, but, as often happens, the fiction of their particular lives tells truths about human life more generally.

In Cairo, Isabel visits the house where Anna lived, and where Anna's father-in-law had dwelt as a Muslim holy man in a shrine set apart from the rest of the building, spending his time praying and weaving cloth on a loom. Anna too learned to weave. The shrine has subsequently been a hermitage for other holy men, and its sacred tomb a place of prayer for pilgrims who come to light candles. But by the time Isabel arrives, there is – we are led to believe – no longer anyone living there, and the shrine is closed. Yet on her arrival at the holy place, she is welcomed by a woman who seems somewhat familiar, dressed in blue and white. The holy man who sits within has a loom, but explains that he cannot always weave because he sometimes has pains in his hands. Each of his hands has a wound at the centre of the palm, which the woman in the blue robe kisses tenderly. The wounds evidently recall the stigmata – the spontaneous wounds that appear on the bodies of certain Christian saints in conformity with the wounds of Christ. The man's name is Sheikh 'Isa, and the serving woman who cares for him addresses the woman in blue as 'Our Lady', a common title for the Virgin Mary, who is venerated by both Christians and Muslims. One of the things that Sheikh 'Isa says to Isabel is, 'Paradise is at the feet of mothers. Remember that.'[5]

After this strange visit, Isabel returns to the shrine at a later date only to find that it has indeed been closed for many years.

The continuity, or solidarity, that exists across several generations of a family and across time and space is described by Soueif through the metaphor of woven fabric, in which strands and colours are twined together to form a single cloth. But the solidarity that she effectively depicts in *The Map of Love* is more mysterious than this. The central character of the novel is Anna, who shares the pages of the book with people of several different religions – Muslims, Christians, Jews and ancient Pagans – and of several different nationalities. Anna's life is revealed to us principally by two of her descendants, the American Isabel and her Egyptian cousin Amal, many decades later, as they piece together their ancestor's letters and diaries. In Soueif's narrative, the boundaries between times, spaces, languages and religions seem permeable, and the characters of the novel move across those boundaries graciously, sometimes by means of artifacts, such as books and pictures, but sometimes in less mundane ways, as in the meeting with the holy man and the Mary-woman at the shrine. Yet the dissolving of boundaries goes beyond even this curious incident.

When Anna first arrives in Egypt, she stays in Cairo; but she longs most of all to visit the Sinai desert. She eventually manages to fulfill her wish, travelling thus to find herself in a land of awe-inspiring majesty, which she describes in the words already quoted from her journal. On coming into full view of the mountains of Sinai, she records the following impression:

> How fitting it is that it should have been here that Moses heard the word of God! For here, … Man – if he is to live – lives perforce so close to Nature and by her Grace, I feel so much closer to the entire mystery of Creation that it would not surprise me at all were I to be vouchsafed a vision or a revelation; indeed it would seem in the very order of things that such an epiphany would happen. I have found myself … offering up prayers …; simple offerings in praise of Him who fashioned all this and who sent me here that I might see it.[6]

In Anna's experience at Sinai, the natural and the supernatural are not radically separate orders, lacking continuity with one another; the experience of one does not imply the exclusion of the other; rather, it is in and through the natural that the supernatural is made manifest. So the traversing, or, indeed, the undermining, of boundaries extends beyond the members of human families, even to encompass a union between the natural and the supernatural. The God who created all things, and who is before and beyond them all, 'naturally' makes himself known by means of that same creation.

In contrast to this, the culture that has become dominant in Europe and North America since the seventeenth century gives most of us a very strong sense of boundaries. We think of human beings as 'individuals', that is, beings unambiguously separated from one another. We think of our own bodies and the rest of the physical world as made up of component parts, each one separate, although co-ordinated and working together. We imagine that each of these individuals or parts has a discrete identity of its own that is quite distinct from other identities. Likewise, we think of times as being clearly distinguished from one another, and places also. We do not suppose that the Jesus and Mary of first-century Palestine might in some way share an identity with, or even be present alongside, Egyptians of the nineteenth and twentieth centuries. We do not usually consider that people who have once inhabited a place and since died might 'really' be present there again. And if mountains, stars or woodlands inspire in us a sense of being in the presence of the sacred, then we probably account for this experience in terms of brain functions or individual psychology, not the indwelling of God in the material world. Yet we should consider the possibility that the maintenance of absolute boundaries between people, between things, between times, between places, and between the natural and the supernatural, may be the imposition of an illusion. It may be that the solidarity of things, one with another, and of God with creation, is a more fundamental truth about the world than is their separation from one another.

If we accept the account of the fictional Anna's experience at Sinai as one which conveys a certain truth about humanity's encounter with the divine, then perhaps it is not surprising if a culture that is at war with nature is a culture that has no place for God. And surely this culture is the one which most Europeans and North Americans now inhabit, and to which the rest of earth and outer space are increasingly subject? Yet it is no more surprising to find that this culture of Godless animosity towards nature grew up in the religious atmosphere of a Christianity that had lost sight of Mary, God's mother. For in Christian teaching, the surety – or at least, the possibility – of union between Deity and matter is given in the conception of the eternal Word of God as a human being in Mary's womb: conceived by her of her own flesh and blood.

For when God became incarnate in Christ, he not only became one man, Jesus of Nazareth, but united himself – at least potentially – to humanity and to the whole created order. And if we believe this, then we must also believe that between human beings, and between humanity and other creatures, there is a solidarity which can override individuation: that it was precisely because Mary's humanity in some way participated in the whole substance of the universe that the humanity of her son could provide the place where God would bind himself to that universe, and thus sanctify it.

So let us go on to consider more fully what it means for Mary to be the Mother of God, and what sort of solidarity might exist between her and the rest of creation.

The Incarnation in the work of salvation

In the liturgy of the Ethiopian Church, a eucharistic prayer addressed to the Virgin Mary begins with the following words:

O Mary, immensity of heaven,
foundation of the earth,

depth of the seas, light of the sun,
beauty of the moon,
splendour of the stars in the heavens ...
Your womb bore God,
before whose majesty man stands in awe.[7]

To some Western ears, these lines may seem unduly extravagant both in the richness of their imagery and in the degree of praise that they lavish upon the Mother of God. Yet they evoke a precise sense of the place of the Blessed Virgin in the order of creation and redemption; and in doing so, they demand that we think again about our attitude towards the cosmos which is our home and the God who made and indwells it, and in whom it dwells. The focus of the Ethiopian prayer is on Mary as Mother of God. And indeed, the doctrine which accords the Virgin this unique status is the most important of the Christian church's Marian teachings.

The belief that the Virgin Mary is the Mother of God is the corollary of the belief that her son, Jesus Christ, is God incarnate. A central tenet of the Christian faith is the doctrine of the Incarnation. This teaches that the Word of God, who is God himself, through whom all things were created, became a part of his own creation when he was conceived, gestated and born of the Virgin Mary. The Word of God is simultaneously the man Jesus of Nazareth because he has a human mother. Theologians have generally agreed that this is an indispensable article of the Christian faith, although the exact reasons for its importance have been disputed. One classical version, however, runs as follows:

God created the world in a state of goodness, as a work of *grace* (something freely given), but sin entered the world when humanity disobeyed the Lord God. This goodness and its loss through human rebellion has traditionally been told through the narrative in which Adam and Eve, the first man and woman, disobey God when they eat the forbidden fruit of the tree of the knowledge of good and evil, in the Garden of Eden, and are expelled to a life of hardship (Genesis 3). This first sin led to men and women being estranged from God, from one another and from the earth with which they struggle for the food, clothing and shelter that sustain them. In theological language, when Adam and Eve ate the forbidden fruit, the consequence was that *nature* fell from *grace*. That is to say, the world as it was created by God (the world of nature) lost some – though not all - of the glory and holiness with which it was originally endowed (that is, grace). This was caused by human sin, but its effect touches all other creatures as well.

What counts here are not the putative first ancestors of the human race, but the representative function that they have always performed. They stand for a humanity which knows that men and women live disordered lives, in which our relationships with God, with one another, and with other creatures – minerals, plants and animals – are often harmful rather than joyful. As the poet Gerard Manley Hopkins writes, 'The world is charged with the grandeur of God. / ... [but] all is seared with trade; bleared, smeared with toil; / And wears man's smudge and shares man's smell: the soil / Is bare now, nor can foot feel, being shod.' Yet, simultaneously with this awareness that the world is awry, Adam and Eve, who once lived in Eden, represent men and women who know that the way the world is now is not how it has to be: indeed, they have confidence that this is not what God wills for it, and even now, that it is not the whole truth. As Hopkins continues: 'And for all this, nature is never spent; / There lives the dearest freshness deep down things.' [8] And the conception and birth of Christ from his mother Mary are cardinal moments in God's redemption of the world from the sin that generates the state of malaise. For God did not wish his creation to continue in its condition of suffering and estrangement from him, and he sent Jesus into the world to save it from sin and death. And Jesus' own death – a violent death by crucifixion – was the only sacrifice which was sufficient to atone for the sins of the world, just as his resurrection from the dead, on the third day following his execution, was the only conquest that could restore humanity to its right relationship with God: that could overcome death itself. The Resurrection constitutes the most fundamental tenet of the Christian faith, and Christ's resurrection and eternal life will be shared by all those who have been redeemed by him, when he returns in judgement on the Last Day and transforms the whole created order into a state of glory.

Now, the reason why the crucifixion and resurrection of Jesus are able to have the redemptive significance which Christians attribute to them lies in Jesus' identity. For Jesus Christ is not only a human being who co-operates with the will of God for the redemption of the world: he is himself divine. Since it was Adam – and with him, all humanity – who sinned, it was necessary that a human being should make good what had been damaged. Yet humanity alone is not capable of restoring the world to that fullness of grace which comes from God alone. And so God redeemed the world by uniting himself to human nature in Jesus, and working the world's redemption as God incarnate, that is, God made flesh.

We can be more specific on this point. In Christian teaching, the One

God is also the Trinity. That is, God is both single and triune, three 'persons' who are nonetheless one. Each person of the Trinity – the Father, the Son (or Word) and the Holy Spirit – is God, and all three persons are present in the action of any one of the three. Thus, God the Father created the world through the eternal Word and in the power of the Holy Spirit; but this is a single action of the one God. In the created world, number is applied to bounded objects conceptualized as separate from one another – three rabbits, twelve currant buns, or two hundred carrots, for example. And if there are three, twelve, or two hundred, then these are not simultaneously one. In God the Creator, however, there is no boundedness – no limit of any kind – and thus no contradiction between the single and the triune nature of the Godhead. The 'threeness' of the Deity is clearly something different from the threeness of the rabbits mentioned above. But this doctrine is too mysterious to be adequately grasped by human understanding, and for that very reason, meditation upon the Trinity provides a safeguard against imagining God to be in our own, or any other, image. The doctrine of the Trinity is the guarantee that humanity cannot comprehend or manipulate the Deity, but must always stand in awe of the God who is before and beyond the boundaries which characterize the created order.

So to be more precise about the Incarnation: since the One God is also the Trinity, it was the eternal Word – or Son – of God, the second person of the Blessed Trinity, who became flesh in Mary's womb for the salvation of the world. Thus, the means by which God chose to save the world from its sins was that he himself should take on human flesh, with all its sensual pleasures and pains; that the Creator should be one with a creature, as an embryo in a woman's entrails; that he who is eternal should take on transience, like the earth, whose substance is shared by human flesh (Genesis 2.7); that he who is immortal should take on mortality, and that he should indeed suffer and die for the sake of his creation.

One of the greatest exponents of the theology of the Incarnation is the fifth-century bishop, Cyril of Alexandria (d.444). Cyril teaches that the Word of God was conceived in Mary's womb in order to consecrate the human race from our very beginnings – that because God himself has been conceived in a woman's body, all human conception may now be sanctified.[9] And because the immortal God united himself to human flesh even in death, he accomplished 'the incorruptibility and imperishability of the flesh ... , first of all in his own body', as we see in his resurrection from the dead, but also for the whole human race. For by uniting himself to human death in Christ, God who is immortal overcame death itself and thus enabled all flesh to be 'set ... beyond death and corruption'.[10] 'In short, he took what was ours to be his very own so that we might have all that was his.'[11]

So Jesus' unique salvific power derives from his identity as both true God and true man, and for this reason, Mary is essential to the Christian account of God and creation. For in the union of God and humanity, it is Mary who imparts the humanity. This belief is expressed in the teaching that Mary conceived Jesus by the power of the Holy Spirit when she was still a virgin (Luke 1.26–38). Eternally begotten of God the Father, Christ was conceived and born on earth of his mother Mary. For this reason she is called by the paradoxical title of *Godbearer* or *Mother of God*. Indeed, it was in order to explain and defend this title for Mary that Cyril of Alexandria wrote his Christology. God of course does not have a beginning: God is from all eternity, with no origin – no parent – outside Godself. But how else are Christians to express the wonder of the Incarnation, whereby God and humanity are perfectly united, if not by the assertion that the human woman who is the mother of Christ is, by that token, the Mother of God? Furthermore, the Catholic, Orthodox and ancient Eastern churches have invariably held that Mary gave her free assent to the conception of Christ. If she had not consented to Gabriel's message, then the world's redemption would not have come about in precisely the manner in which it did: the redeemer would not have been the Jesus of Nazareth who in fact is God incarnate. So Mary is not only a physical, but also a moral, agent in the world's salvation.

The aptness of the Ethiopian prayer now starts to become apparent. For God the Father created all things – from the breathtaking galaxy of the clear night sky, down to the softest damp blades of green moss – and he did this work as the Trinity, through the eternal Word, in the power of the Holy Spirit. Yet this same God, the eternal Word, in some incomprehensible manner was also held and nurtured in the tiny space of Mary's belly. Small wonder, then, that the greatest marvels of the material world are called upon to evoke a sense of her incomparable spiritual grandeur!

The Maybush

In the Western church, as well as in the East, poets have wondered at the miracle of Mary's conceiving and gestating of the Lord of the universe. For example, the sixth-century Latin poet, Venantius Fortunatus, wrote the mystical hymn 'Quem terra, pontus, aethera', which begins:

Him whom earth, sea and air
cherish, adore and proclaim

as he rules the threefold order,
Mary's sealed chamber bears.[12]

However, a belief in Mary's intimate involvement with the fabric of the material world has been expressed more commonly in the myriad of folk beliefs which associate her directly with the elements of 'earth, sea and air', and especially with earth and water. Throughout the Christian world, there are rocks and springs which are sacred to the Virgin, as well as stars, flowers and trees.

The Spanish shrine of Nuestra Señora del Rocío, Our Lady of the Dew, at Almonte in Huelva, is in several respects typical of shrines associated with the natural world. The legend of its foundation tells the story of a huntsman on horseback. Approaching the woods near Almonte,

> his interest and curiosity were stirred when he heard something like the bark of a dog and saw a mysterious movement among a tangle of thornbushes. With great difficulty he guided his horse through the high grass, while small animals scurried away and birds fluttered overhead. His interest was no longer in hunting, but in following an inner prompting to travel deeper into the forest. Presently he saw a large bush and atop it a lily nestled among a cluster of thorns. Then, looking aside, he saw a vision of the Queen of Heaven. ... Dressed in a linen tunic of pale green, she said nothing. She mysteriously disappeared, leaving behind a statue of remarkable beauty.[13]

On seeing the vision, the hunter dismounted, and on finding the statue, with great joy, he decided to carry it on his shoulders back to the town.

When he arrived, he was very tired after the exertion and fell asleep. But when he woke up, the statue had disappeared. Being distressed by its absence, he went with others from the town back to the tree of the apparition, and found beside it the statue, covered with dew and in its original place. A chapel was therefore built at the apparition site, and the trunk of the thorn was used as the pedestal for the statue.

Whit Monday, which falls in May or June, is the most important feast day for devotions in honour of Our Lady of the Dew.

Many shrines of the Virgin Mary have founding narratives which tell of a statue being discovered in a wild, or semi-wild, place, of the statue's being removed to the local town, and of its returning of its own accord to the site of its discovery. This indicates that the holy place has been designated by

God, or by the Blessed Virgin in accordance with God's will, and may not be determined by ordinary human choice. The stories seem to say that men and women must recognize their dependence upon powers that are greater than their own, and ultimately, of course, upon God. Moreover, the fact that Our Lady's devotees are forced to make a pilgrimage away from the town to find her in the woods, and there to venerate her in a tree, suggests that it is in the world of 'nature', rather than civilization, that Mary and her divine Son ask to be encountered: as though we must remember our vulnerability in the face of natural forces, and through these, our dependence upon their Maker.

Sacred thorn bushes are found at many Marian shrines. At Aránzazu, in the Spanish Basque country, the image of Our Lady of the Hawthorn is still venerated on a tree trunk;[14] whilst in Britain, the legends of Glastonbury likewise associate Mary with a sacred thorn. According to ancient tradition, Joseph of Arimathea, who had given the tomb for Christ's burial, came to Somerset, and at Glastonbury built the first Christian church on the island of Britain, dedicating the building to St Mary. The site on which the church was built later became the Lady Chapel of Glastonbury Abbey, which held a miraculous image of the Virgin that was a focus of pilgrimage for many centuries. The tradition of St Joseph also maintains that he struck his staff into the ground, where it took root as a thorn tree which still blossoms at midwinter – that is, at the time when the Church celebrates Mary's giving birth to Christ.

In general, however, hawthorn and whitethorn are the trees which herald the arrival of summer. Hawthorn is the May tree, decorated and danced around as it buds on May morning, by revellers welcoming the voluptuous greening of the earth again after the brown months of winter. May morning is the time when Jack in the Green appears, covered in foliage, as though to represent the spirit of the awakening land.[15] And in Catholic Christianity, the month of May is especially consecrated to the Mother of God. May processions, and other joyful devotions in her honour, mark this out as Mary's month.

The earliest indication of Mary's association with May comes from a martyrology, or list of saints' days, from eighth-century Ireland, which records that there was a feast of St Mary at the beginning of the month.[16] In modern times, it has been the custom in many places for people to put up May altars – temporary shrines to the Virgin – in their homes.

The implicit reason for Mary's association with Maytime is not hard to see. When Mary consents to become the mother of Christ and conceives him in her womb, as we have already seen, new life starts to be restored to all creation. So the month of May, with the return of summer, is the seasonal realization of a mystery that is also historical and celestial. As the mother of the author of all living things, Mary's presence is sensed amongst created beings in their own generation of new life. And the life that is present in them is a participation in the life of God, who himself is united to the life of all creatures through binding himself to Mary's flesh and blood. In one of her many hymns, the poet and visionary, St Hildegard of Bingen (1098–1179), addresses the Virgin with the words, 'Hail, O greenest branch'; and in a celebration of the abundant life that comes forth from the mother of Christ, the metaphor of the branch is extended to proclaim that the birds of the air build their nests in her.[17]

Yet the new life of spring has arisen from the mire of decay, and will in turn, sooner or later, grow old and pass away in the natural course of change and death. Things which are born will inevitably die, and this truth is not forgotten in the popular traditions of May morning. Young men and women would go out into the woods on May eve, and return in the early hours with May branches to give to householders. Typically, the traditional songs that the Mayers sang on their rounds include verses such as the following:

> O wake up, you, wake up, pretty maid,
> And let the Maybush in,
> Or we shall be gone ere tomorrow morn
> And you will have none within.

> The life of man is but a span,
> He's cut down like a flower.
> Oh, make no delay! He is here today
> And he's vanished all in an hour.

> And when you're dead and in your grave
> And covered in the cold, cold clay,
> The worms, they will eat your flesh, good man,
> And your bones, they will waste away.

The boundary between life and death is as fragile as the mayblossom, and is crossed as easily as the flower is crushed.

Yet in the Christian doctrine of the Word's becoming human, it is precisely this passing, corruptible matter which God cherishes and makes his own. God has bound himself to this world in its decay and mortality, so that things which are transient by nature will be made immortal by grace. This blessing upon frailty is accomplished in the Incarnation, Crucifixion and Resurrection, but after these, bears its first fruit in the assumption of the Virgin Mary into heaven. The doctrine of the Assumption teaches that, after the end of her earthly life, Mary's body did not rot away in the earth, but was reunited with her soul 'in heavenly glory', so that she has already achieved the state of bliss which awaits others at the end of time. This was a popular Christian belief from early centuries, and was commemorated in a feast day, on 15th August, from at least the seventh century.[18] In 1950, Pope Pius XII made it an official teaching of the Catholic Church. In the prayers that are read at Mass and in the Church's daily prayers on the Feast of the Assumption, we find a suggestion as to the motive for God's giving this privilege to Mary, namely, that the body which alone bore God incarnate would not be allowed to know decay. Since God united himself to mortal flesh, the particular flesh to which he united himself is the first to be delivered into a state of immortality. Yet by becoming the son of Mary, the Son of God honoured and redeemed not just the body and soul of his mother, but all other perishable flesh as well. So the privilege that is given to Mary is a token, and the first fulfillment, of God's desire to give glory to all humanity – and, as I shall go on to contend, to all the living and dying creatures which constitute and sustain us, and the many more with whom we share our elemental matter.

The Incarnation for the sake of creation's glory

The fact that God's incarnation in a human being is central to Christian teaching might suggest that Christianity is unduly preoccupied with humanity, to the neglect of the rest of creation – animal, vegetable and mineral. Yet from the examples of popular devotion already cited, it can be seen that the incarnation of God in Jesus Christ has not always been interpreted in this way; on the contrary, it has been, and should be, understood as sanctifying in some measure every creature God has made. But this understanding is sustained only by taking proper account of the contribution made by Mary, the Mother of God; for without her, we are in danger of straying into a view of God and Christ that gives unbridled supremacy to human beings.

So when God became flesh, why did he take the form of a human being, rather than some other creature? One answer to this – that it was necessary for the world's redemption – has already been given. But this may be only a part of the answer, and possibly not the most important part, since the question as to why God's incarnation took human form was raised and discussed by the master theologians of the Middle Ages, who came up with a variety of arguments by way of reply. Amongst a number of possible answers suggested by the medieval scholastics, we find the suggestion that the human being is a microcosm, and thus provided a means by which God could unite himself to the entire creation and perfect it.[19] So let us consider what is entailed in this claim.

The doctrine of the human person as microcosm is an ancient one,[20] which remained popular until the seventeenth century.[21] It holds that the cosmos, or the universe, is in some way contained or reflected in miniature in each man or woman. The polymathic abbess, Hildegard of Bingen, for example, writing of the creation of the world, exclaims, 'O human, look at the human being! For human beings hold together within themselves heaven and earth and other things created, and are one form; and within them everything is concealed.'[22] Thus, for example, the human being may be understood to consist of both material and spiritual aspects, unlike, say, rocks, which are matter, or angels, who are primarily spirits. The various parts of the human body, and their arrangement, are often seen as analogous to the various parts and specific ordering of the universe. Hildegard writes of the five planets (all the planets that were then known to humanity): 'as a human's five senses hold the body together, so too these five planets hold the sun together and are its ornament.'[23] Conversely, the cosmos is typically understood to be a living organism. So the heart, upon which human life depends, may be seen as the sun of the human body, since the sun gives life to the world, and the sun in turn may be viewed as the heart of the known universe.

The correspondence between the human person and the cosmos is thus one of substance, as well as likeness of form. Hildegard writes:

In the way that the elements ... hold the world together so they are also the fastening of the human body. Their perfusion and operating in human beings is apportioned in such a way that they are held together. This is similar to the way the elements perfuse the world and affect it. Fire, air, water, and earth are present in human beings, who consist of them. For they have warmth from fire, breath from air, blood from water, and flesh from earth.[24]

Furthermore, this analogy with, and participation in, the life of the universe means that human destiny is bound up with the rest of creation not only in the obvious respects whereby, for example, drought and flood, good harvest or clean water affect human welfare, but also in more subtle ways. For instance, the movements of stars and planets can favour good or bad fortune for human beings either individually or collectively. And in this type of understanding of microcosm and macrocosm, the converse may also be true. That is, it may be believed that specifically human action, such as the performance of religious rituals, can have a beneficent or malign effect on other parts of the natural order.

In the understanding of the human person as microcosm, then, it is implicitly assumed that there is a solidarity between humanity and other aspects of the natural world. Humanity, the earth and the stars are bound together by visible and invisible ties. Moreover, God too is included in this bond. To return to the example of the sun: in Christian tradition, the sun is supremely a symbol of Christ. Christ is known as the Sun of Righteousness; Christian churches have commonly been orientated eastwards, towards the rising sun, as a sign of looking for Christ's return; and Christmas, the feast of Christ's birth, is celebrated at midwinter, when the sun is 'reborn', beginning its ascent in the heavens after its winter decline. The correspondence between Christ, the sun and the human heart means that the ground already exists on which the Word of God can become incarnate in both the human person and the rest of creation. A certain commonality between God, humanity and the universe is, as it were, natural. So medieval theologians could argue that when God united himself to one man, Jesus of Nazareth, he was simultaneously uniting himself to the whole cosmos. Indeed, they could argue that it was only in order to sanctify and glorify the universe that God the Creator chose a human being, rather than some other creature, to be the subject of his paradoxical identity with the creation. So the human being has a uniquely important place in this account of the Incarnation, but it is an importance which renders the human condition in a certain respect subservient to the welfare of creation as a whole, since the unique constitution of the human person as microcosm means that, in addition to the task of allowing God to accomplish our own salvation, men and women also have to assist all other creatures in their attainment of perfection.

Now, according to this exposition of the mystery of the Incarnation, in order to sanctify the universe, God was conceived as an embryo and grew as a human being in the womb of the Virgin Mary, and it was by taking his humanity specifically from her that God in Christ entered into solidarity with all creatures. On the one hand, then, the microcosmic humanity of Jesus is assured by his having a human mother, Mary, and she is thereby the guarantee that God has bound himself to the most minute corner and the most vast expanse of his creation. Conversely, we might suspect that one danger entailed in thinking about, or representing, Christ's humanity apart from his mother is that he will appear as the divine man who has lordship over other creatures but is not seen to be dependent upon or to participate in them in any way. The Ethiopian prayer's use of cosmic imagery for Mary signifies that Christ is grounded in the material universe, and at the same time, that the material world, in the person of Mary, is exalted by God's presence within it in the person of the Son to whom she gave flesh within her body.

Creation glorified in the Mother of God

Two arguments have now been outlined to account for the incarnation of God in Christ. They do not have to be mutually exclusive, but there is a significant difference with regard to God's 'motive' in the two accounts. Whereas the first argument to explain why the Incarnation took place in human, rather than some other, form referred back to the sin of Adam – that is, to human wickedness – the second argument was concerned with the perfection, or glorification, of the whole creation, and God's union with it. The first argument sees the Incarnation solely as a response to human sin: it is God's means of redeeming the world from evil, which is to say, of putting right a creation – and in particular, a human race – that has gone wrong. The argument from the microscosm, however, is not primarily concerned with redemption from sin, but with the perfection of a creation that is already seen as good. In Genesis 1 it is stated clearly that everything made by God is made in a state of goodness, but Christians have disagreed as to the extent to which this goodness is undermined by human sin. If the Incarnation is understood to be primarily an exercise in rescuing a fallen world, there is a tendency to focus both on humanity and on sin, since these are the main elements in the Fall. If, however, the Incarnation is understood to be primarily an exercise in perfecting a good creation, then one's emphasis is likely to be on precisely that: the goodness of creation.

A notable champion of the view that redemption was not the primary motive for the Incarnation was the great Franciscan theologian, John Duns Scotus (1265–1304).[25] Scotus argued that God would have accomplished the incarnation in Christ even if Adam (i.e., humanity) had not sinned, because the purpose of it was the glorification of God's creation, that is, the bringing of all things into union with him. This was expressed in temporal language, to the effect that the Incarnation was 'previsioned' before the sin of Adam was foreseen. Once Adam had sinned, the Incarnation did then provide the remedy for evil, but the drama which moves from fall to redemption takes place within a broader framework that begins with creation and culminates in glorification. Furthermore, this destiny to glory applies not only to humanity, but to the whole of creation – hence the argument of the microcosm, cited above.

Other theologians, such as the medieval Majorcan Ramon Llull (1232–1316), or the modern German Karl Rahner, have pointed out that if the Incarnation in Jesus was ordained 'from before the sin of Adam was foreseen', then it must follow that Mary likewise was predestined to be the Mother of God in the same act, since the particular incarnation of God in Jesus depends upon Mary giving him his human nature.[26] Again, the idea of Mary's predestination to be the Mother of God has frequently been associated with a strong belief in the goodness of God's creation.[27] An explicit association between Mary and the foundations of the cosmos is made by many Catholic writers (some of whose work will be considered below); but the work of the highly influential French spiritual writer, St John Eudes (1601–80), author of *The Admirable Heart of Mary*,[28] is particularly relevant in relation to the motif of the microcosm.

Devotion to the heart of Mary was a recent introduction to Catholic spiritual life in the seventeenth century, and John Eudes was its first major proponent. In effect, he presents Mary's heart as a representative figure for her whole person, and he understands Mary in turn to have a close correspondence with the cosmos. Eudes follows Aristotle (and many medieval teachers) in giving an account of the three parts of the human soul: 'the vegetative soul, which is similar in nature to that of plants, ... the sensitive life, which we have in common with animals ... [and] the intellectual life, like that of angels.'[29] Thus, all the orders of life are contained in the human being. Jean Eudes' account of the universe likewise follows a triadic (or trinitarian) pattern:

> The infinite power of God has divided this great universe into three different states or orders, namely, the state of nature, the state of grace and the state of glory. ... whatever is in the order of nature is an image of the things belonging to the order of grace, and whatever

belongs to the order of nature and grace is a figure [i.e., reflection, or foreshadowing] of what is to be seen in the state of glory.[30]

The realms of the natural and the supernatural are thus continuous with one another, and one can see a certain correspondence between the structure of the human soul and that of the universe as a whole. When Eudes comes to write of Mary's heart, he also draws distinctions under three headings: her 'corporeal heart', her 'spiritual heart', and her 'divine heart'. The corporeal heart, he says, is not only the principle of her own earthly life, but also produced the blood of which Christ's body was formed. It is the source of the material life of Christ in the womb.[31] The spiritual heart is the noblest portion of the soul; it is made in the image of God, and by grace is able to participate in the divine nature.[32] In Mary, that image is untarnished, and the participation, or divinization, is as full as possible. And finally, the divine heart is that aspect of Mary which is concerned directly with her divine motherhood – with the fact that she is the Mother of God. Christ, says Eudes, is the heart of God the Father, and he is also the heart of his earthly mother. That is to say, the Word of God is not only the Son of both God the Father and the human Mary, but is also the heart of both. He lives in every part of her, both physical and spiritual.[33] The divine heart therefore ties Mary immediately to the life of the Blessed Trinity.

It can be seen that the threefold division of Mary's heart does not correspond to the threefold division of the human soul, since the properties of the vegetative and sensitive are subsumed under the 'corporeal', whilst the 'divine heart' is proper to Mary alone in virtue of her being the Mother of God. Yet the correspondence between Mary's heart and the three orders of the universe is at least as good as that between those three orders and that of the ordinary human soul, with the corporeal heart corresponding to the state of nature, the spiritual heart to the state of grace, and the divine heart to the state of glory . And indeed, Jean Eudes compares Mary to the cosmos in some detail. For example, he claims that Mary's heart corresponds to the sun: 'the sun, which is truly the heart of the visible world, and the most beautiful and glowing gem of nature, gives us ... only a very faint shadow of our heavenly Sun, the Heart of the Mother of God.'[34] As the sun is the source of life for the earth, so the heart is the source of life for the human body, and Mary's heart for the world which is redeemed in her son. Moreover, it is not Mary who is a reflection of creation, but creation that is a reflection of Mary. Thus, the first earth, from which Adam was made, is an imperfect image of the second earth, who is Mary from whom Christ was made. Correspondingly, then, other aspects of creation are images of Mary's glory or virtues, so that the mountains, for example, reflect the 'perfections of the Sovereign Lady of the Universe'.[35] And the sea, which has long been associated with Mary in popular devotion,[36] is a figure for the vastness of Mary's purity and miracles.[37]

So Jean Eudes understands the human person as a being that corresponds to the whole order of creation, and the heart of Mary to be, as it were, the perfection of the microcosm and the archetype of the macrocosm: creation in the state of glory. In her, furthermore, God is fully united to creation, and he seeks union with other human souls. Addressing the reader, Eudes writes: 'Our Lord Jesus Christ, who is the Heart of the Eternal Father, willed to become the Heart or life-principle of His Most Blessed Mother, and He likewise wills to become the Heart of your own life.'[38] This union would not be possible if there were not some kind of commonality (be it one of substance, of image or of some other kind) between God and the human soul, and for Jean Eudes, that commonality binds God, humanity and all creation in a manner whose template is found in the Blessed Virgin, in her unique relationships with God and with the universe.

Solidarity and the individual

As we have already seen, St Cyril of Alexandria contends that when the Word of God became incarnate in the Virgin Mary, he united himself not simply to the one man Jesus of Nazareth, who is uniquely both God and human, but, by extension, to the whole human race, and even to the rest of creation, and thereby redeemed it. Indeed, this teaching is integral to the Christology and soteriology (the doctrine of salvation) of the early Christian teachers. In the fourth century, the theologian Gregory of Nazianzus wrote, 'That which has not been assumed cannot be restored; it is what is united with God that is saved.'[39] This means that if God did not really take upon himself ('assume') the human condition in Christ's saving work, then that work has not really saved humanity. This view was put forward by other Church Fathers of the same period, so that it became a sort of leitmotif amongst those theologians who defended the doctrine that Christ was fully and inseparably both human and divine. For modern people, however, there may appear to be a metaphysical problem here. For, as I have already noted, we tend to think of human beings primarily as 'individuals', that is, as essentially separate from one another, which means that it is not clear how God's union with any one human being extends to incorporate others. Why should God's taking flesh of Mary and becoming human in Jesus of Nazareth necessarily entail some sort of union with other men and women? The early Christian writers do not explain how this occurs; and the reason why they do not explain it is that they start off with an entirely different anthropology, or doctrine of the human person, from ours. Rather than thinking of human beings and other creatures primarily as individuals, they think of everything as being essentially in solidarity, or continuity, with everything else. So when God binds himself to one man in his mother's flesh, he thereby binds himself to all those beings who are born of woman's flesh, or made of the dust of the earth.

This solidarity between creatures may be accounted for in different ways, and Cyril does not indicate clearly what he believes to be its character. We have seen above that it can take the form of the human person as microcosm, but this itself includes ideas of solidarity both by formal *likeness* – the human person as sharing a similar image and structure to that of the universe – and by *substance* – the human person as made of the same elements as the universe – and either of these on its own may account for the solidarity of humanity with other creatures. For the purpose of the present argument, it does not greatly matter what is the precise character of the continuity which exists between the humanity of Christ and other beings, only that God's taking flesh from Mary guarantees his solidarity with the material universe.

To understand the immense significance of this, it will help to consider some of the differences between the typically modern (and originally Western and Northern) understanding of the human person, and that of more ancient cultures. And to do this, let us turn first to the sixteenth century, a period of enormous cultural change in Western Europe.

In the year 1543, Andrew Vesalius published his work *De humani corporis fabrica*, 'Concerning the fabric of the human body', a work which, with hindsight, is judged to be of crucial importance in the development of the study of human anatomy. It consists of 700 pages, with 300 engravings showing dissections of the human body. According to the medical sociologist, David Le Breton, Vesalius' work marks a cardinal point in the transformation of European attitudes to the human body and to the world which the body inhabits.[40] Le Breton argues that the body – that is, the human body – as the concept is currently employed, is a concomitant or component part of modern individualism, and did not exist as such in other cultures before they were subject to European influence, or, indeed, in medieval Europe before the rise of individualism in the fifteenth century.

The body, as it is now understood, is something possessed by an apparently immaterial subject or actor, the 'I'. Thus, we say, 'I *have* a body.' The body is treated – most notably, in modern medicine – as though it is distinct from the person to whom it belongs; and the body in turn is the principle of separation between one person and another. It is managed in such a way as to maintain boundaries between individuals. For example, modern people are very guarded about whom they touch and who may stand close to them. Le Breton argues that in most other cultures, bodily parts and flesh are perceived as being points of union or continuity with other people and with other aspects of the physical world. In many cultures, it is normal for people conducting a conversation to take hold of one another whilst they are talking.

The notion that human beings are connected to their physical surroundings may be expressed in quite sophisticated terms. We have already seen the European example of the microcosm, and Le Breton cites examples from African cultures also.[41] In this kind of view of the human person, physical and spiritual elements are always integrated, and in some cases are inseparable or even indistinguishable.

I have already referred to the example from the Hebrew Scriptures of the teaching that Adam is made from the soil of the earth. This is, amongst other things, an assertion of humanity's solidarity and continuity with the rest of the physical world. We are of the same stuff as this earth and all that grows on it. So our materiality is what joins us to other beings, not what separates us.

A more secular example of the way in which people have understood themselves to be in continuity with the world around them may be found in folk stories, which tell of humans being turned to stone, or into animals and fairy-folk. These indicate an understanding of the human person whereby the boundaries between the human and the non-human are perceived to be weak or permeable. The base matter which once constituted a prince may equally well constitute a frog: it is the form that is inconstant, not the substance. Indeed, material substance is precisely what princes and frogs have in common with one another.[42]

At the same time as the human person is seen to be in continuity with the rest of the cosmos, moreover, there is a shared identity between the human person and the person's flesh. Le Breton contends that the identity of the flesh with the person is seen in the cults of saints. Marks found on a saint's bodily organs may be taken to reveal his or her sanctity of soul. Likewise, touching the relics of a holy man or woman places one in the very presence of the saint. A relic is not just a memento or keepsake. It is not even that the part merely stands for the whole: the part actually incarnates the whole, as when Jean Eudes writes of Mary's heart as though it were Mary herself. For the same reason, General Franco took possession of the relics of St Teresa of Avila, because to be in contact with the saint's mortal remains, or even some part of them, is to be in the saint's company, and so enables the possessor to seek the saint's protection with particular efficacy.

Thus, in this worldview and its accompanying practices, body and soul are one person; furthermore, that one person shares a solidarity of substance or of form with the rest of creation; and, as I suggested by the example of the relationship between Christ and the sun, or between Mary and the cosmos, all these things are sanctified by their Creator and Redeemer.

Under these circumstances, then, it is not surprising that for hundreds of years the Catholic Church forbade the anatomical dissection of human bodies, or permitted it only under the strictest ecclesiastical supervision. That supervision would include the saying of prayers for the repose of the soul of the person being dissected, and the reassembly of the person's bodily parts for a funeral Mass and burial. The anatomist and his assistant had to be present at the requiem Mass. The Church's strictures were plainly an attempt to respect the integrity of body and soul, the sanctity of the human person, and the place of the human person within the created order. The human person is destined for resurrection and immortality, not for the cold steel of the anatomist's knife.

All this gradually came to be disrupted and undermined with those social changes that led some people to start thinking of themselves primarily as 'individuals', that is, individuated beings cut off from the society which they inhabited, from the natural world, and even from their own bodies. And this is a development which Le Breton associates also with the split between 'learned' culture, which fostered individualism, and 'popular' culture, which in some cases still retains a more ancient understanding of the human person and their place in the cosmos.

What the learned Vesalius did was, in effect, to take the human body out of the social and natural environment in which it had lived, as though it were unconnected to the earth or to other human beings, placing it on a profane dissection table, and then to handle it as dead matter unconnected to a human soul. And is this not what modern people frequently mean when we use the word 'body': a collection of organs co-ordinated with one another by mechanical and chemical processes? It is bereft of social, ecological or sacred significance. Furthermore, as has often been noted, 1543 was not only the year when Vesalius's anatomical dissections were published, but it was also the year of the publication of Copernicus' *De Revolutionibus*, which first put forward the theory that the sun, and not the earth, was at the centre of the universe. This was contrary to the Church's usual interpretation of the Scriptures, and was the contention which eventually led Galileo into trouble with the Inquisition. So not only were human beings claiming the right to dissect and analyse the microcosm, independently of sacred authority, but simultaneously, they were asserting the right to become intellectual lords of the cosmos itself. The heliocentric theory of the universe manifests just the same detachment of humanity from nature as is seen in anatomical dissections of human bodies. An astronomer who assumes that the earth is at the centre of the universe is, after all, just describing the world as he or she sees it. Copernicus, on the other hand, by placing the sun at the centre of his planetary scheme was asserting that the human mind could move way beyond such straighforward observation and behave *as though* it were located outside the solar system altogether. This intellectual leap surely indicates an extraordinary estrangement of the human thinker from their environment. Moreover, the human mind now occupied a position that had previously been occupied only by God, whilst the universe itself was being evacuated of sacred meaning. Evidently, then, attitudes to humanity and to the material world continued to mirror each other, but where both had previously been considered familiar and sacred, each was now becoming alien and profane.[43]

This change in Western culture's understanding of the human person and the natural world is of great significance in relation to several aspects of Christian doctrine and devotion, not least, regarding the Blessed Virgin Mary. In the medieval romance *The Quest of the Holy Grail*,[44] the knights of King Arthur go in search of the Grail, that is, the chalice that bore Christ's blood. There is some ambiguity as to the vessel's precise identity. It may be that which Christ used at the Last Supper, when he instituted the sacrament of the Eucharist, in which the wine becomes his blood through consecration; or it may be the goblet in which Christ's blood was collected after he was pierced through the side as he hung on the cross. Either way, the Grail is the vessel which carried the blood of the Lord. Significantly, commentators on *The Quest* have noted that in the narrative, the act of coming into the presence of the Grail is treated as though it is the same thing as coming into the presence of Christ himself. To be allowed to see the Grail is to be allowed to enter the presence of the Lord.[45]

This is surely because the Lord's previous presence in the Grail has imparted to it something of himself. So from this point of view, the vessel's physical boundary no longer counts because its sacred occupant has, simply by being there, infused it with his continuing presence.

If this is true of the Grail, then *a fortiori*, it is true of the Mother of God. Not only has God incarnate dwelt in her, but his very human substance is from her, and for some months they were, quite literally, one flesh. Much elevated devotion to Mary has arisen not because people have mistakenly attributed to her qualities which properly belong to Christ, but because her unique participation in Christ's identity means that she continues, in a limited measure, to share in that identity.

Now, when we think about beings participating in one another, or sharing an identity, there is a philosophical difference between asserting that such participation occurs amongst created beings – such as humanity and the cosmos – and asserting that such participation occurs between God and a creature – such as Christ and the Grail, or Christ and his mother. If we can assert that distinct creatures, including human beings, can share an identity, then this does imply that the modern concept of the individual is mistaken. In the case of God, however, who has no limitations or boundaries of any kind, there is no logical objection to believing both that human beings, or chalices, are primarily discrete individuals, and that God may participate in, and sanctify, them in an extraordinary manner. However, Le Breton makes a comment that is extremely pertinent to this point. He observes that in the creation of the modern Western understanding,

> the individual marks himself off from those who are like him. Simultaneously, the withdrawal, then the abandonment of the theological vision of nature leads the individual to think of the world which surrounds him as a pure, indifferent form: an ontologically empty form which only the human craftsman now has the authority to fashion. ... The individuation of humanity goes hand in hand with the desacralization of nature.[46]

It is as though our ability to sense the sacred – our ability to sense God's presence in things – goes hand in hand with our having a more general awareness of the participation of beings in one another by identity. If we cannot perceive some fundamental continuity within the material order, then we cannot perceive the unity of spirit and matter, and neither can we perceive the unity of God with God's creatures. We either treat the world as essentially made up of component parts, or else we treat it as essentially consisting of common properties; and if we do the former, then we shall have great difficulty in understanding how God can be bound in to the creation. To believe that God is truly present in Christ thus depends upon our ability to believe that when Jesus was conceived by Mary, he was fundamentally united to the rest of the world, from which it then follows that God himself participated in that wider union. And by the same token, God's unique presence in Christ cannot be neatly cut off from the mother whose flesh he made his own, unless we are to abandon our ability to discern God's presence in the material world at all. Christian orthodoxy therefore seems to require of believers that they adopt a radically critical attitude to all those aspects of modernity which depend upon the notion that people and things are primarily 'individuals'.

Moreover, there is more than one point at which there is a tension between Christian Marian doctrine and the modern 'body'. The history of anatomical dissection is connected not merely with a desacralization of the natural world, but positively with evil, in the sense of criminality. During the Renaissance period, it was often the case that the only bodies available for dissection were those of criminals who had been hanged and were left on the gibbet in a public place. During this period, and down to far more recent times, the shortage of bodies for dissection led anatomists and medical students to steal bodies from graveyards. Popular mythology holds that Vesalius did just this.[47]

So what image could stand in sharper contrast to that of the human person mutilated on the dissection table than that of the Virgin Mary assumed into heaven? Where the dissected person may be a criminal, or is treated as a criminal, the Virgin is sinless and is honoured. Where the dissected body is cut up into pieces of flesh, the Virgin is assumed in her entirety, 'body and soul'. And where the dissected body is dead, the Virgin is living. And this contrast is not thrown up randomly; because if we ask the question, 'What is it to be fully and properly human?', the answer given by Catholicism implicitly takes the form of teachings and other practices concerning the Blessed Virgin. In Mary, we see what God intends us all to be – and more than this, we see what God intends for the whole of creation. If Mary is the Godbearer, then does this not mean the very fabric of the universe in some measure has the capacity to be the dwelling place of Deity? And, as should be clear by now, the relationship between Mary's Godbearing and the rest of creation is not only a symbolic one. It is because of the solidarity which exists between her and all other things that her conception and gestating of God incarnate can redeem the whole world. But note that the truth of Mary's Godbearing depends upon the world being one of solidarity and continuity more radically than it is one of separated individuals. If we are fundamentally individuals, then there is no reason why the incarnation of God in one man, Jesus of Nazareth, should make much difference to anyone else. The doctrine of salvation depends upon the belief that human beings are fundamentally of one stuff, in solidarity with one another, so that, when God became incarnate in Jesus of Nazareth, he was taking upon himself not just the humanity of one man, but the very fabric of the cosmos, in the flesh of his mother Mary. The history of the Christian Church suggests that if we imagine Christ to be quite separate from Mary, we run the risk of seeing him only as an 'individual', disconnected from the rest of the world, and not as its inner life of renewal and sanctification.

We have now seen that Mary's solidarity with the whole created order is integral to the world's redemption and glorification. We have also seen that Mary corresponds to, and even shares an identity with, that which is signified by 'the deep' in Genesis 1.2, that is, with the foundations of the material creation. This suggests that Mary's participation in the material creation is more fundamental, and perhaps more pervasive, than that of any other creature – that her participation in other creatures derives from a prior presence in the very stuff of which the world is formed. In the next chapter, we shall go on to consider more closely the character of Mary's association with the foundations of the cosmos.

Notes

1 Gillett, H.M., *Shrines of Our Lady in England and Wales*, Samuel Walker, London, 1957, 61–2.

2 The Catholic church in Cardigan has re-established the shrine about half a mile from the original site.

3 Boss, S.J., *Empress and Handmaid: On Nature and Gender in the Cult of the Virgin Mary*, Cassell, London, 2000, 82–5.

4 Soueif, A., *The Map of Love*, Bloomsbury Publishing, London, 2000, 210–11.

5 Soueif, *op. cit.*, 291–300.

6 Soueif, *op. cit.*, 213.

7 Berselli, C. and Gharib, G. (eds), *In Praise of Mary: Hymns from the First Millennium of the Eastern and Western Churches* (trans. P. Jenkins), St Paul Publications, Slough, 1981, 80.

8 Hopkins, G. M. *Poems and Prose* (ed. W.H. Gardner), Penguin, Harmondsworth, 1963, 27.

9 'Third Letter of Cyril to Nestorius', from the documents of the Council of Ephesus (431), in Tanner SJ, N.P., (ed.), *Decrees of the Ecumenical Councils*, Sheed & Ward, London / Georgetown University Press, Washington, 1990, Vol. 1, 58.

10 St Cyril of Alexandria, *On the Unity of Christ* (trans. J. A. McGuckin) St Vladimir's Seminary Press, Crestwood, New York, 1995, 57.

11 St Cyril, *op. cit.*, 59.

12 This hymn is best known in the translation by J.M. Neale, whose first line is 'The God whom earth and sea and sky'.

13 Carroll, J., *Miraculous Images of Our Lady*, Tan Books, Rockford, Illinois, 1993, 422–3.

14 Pannet, R., *Marie au Buisson Ardent*, Editions S.O.S., Paris, 1982, 104; photograph by Helmuth Nils Loose in Rahner SJ, K., *Ignatius of Loyola* (trans. R. Ockenden), Collins, London, 1979, picture 12.

15 Anderson, W. and Hicks, C., *Green Man: The Archetype of our Oneness with the Earth*, HarperCollins, London and San Francisco, 1990, 8–13; for a survey of British May customs and their possible origins, see Hutton, R., *The Stations of the Sun*, Oxford University Press, Oxford, 1996, 226–43.

16 *The Martyrology of Tallaght*, discussed in O'Loughlin, T., 'The cult of Mary within the structures of human time: A reading of some early mediaeval Irish martyrologies', in *Maria: A Journal of Marian Studies* 3:2, Continuum, London, 2003, and Clayton, M., *The Cult of the Virgin Mary in Anglo-Saxon England*, Cambridge University Press, Cambridge, 1990, 32–3 and 40–1.

17 Text given in Newman, B., *Sister of Wisdom: St. Hildegard's Theology of the Feminine*, Scolar Press, Aldershot, 1987, 279.

18 Shoemaker, S.J., *Ancient Traditions of the Virgin Mary's Dormition and Assumption*, Oxford University Press, Oxford, 2002, 121. See also p.59, for evidence of an earlier celebration of the feast on different dates.

19 Thomas Aquinas, *Commentary on the Sentences of Peter Lombard*, Book III, dist.2, q.1, a.1, resp.; quoted in Manteau-Bonamy OP, H.-M., *Maternité Divine et Incarnation: Etude historique et doctrinale de Saint Thomas à nos jours*, Librairie Philosophique J. Vrin, Paris, 1949, 27.

20 Wright, M.R., *Cosmology in Antiquity*, Routledge, London, 1995, 56–74.

21 Funkenstein, A., *Theology and the Scientific Imagination from the*

Middle Ages to the Seventeenth Century, Princeton University Press, Princeton, New Jersey, 1986, 28.

22 Hildegard of Bingen, *On Natural Philosophy and Medicine: Selections from* Cause et Cure (trans. M. Berger), Boydell and Brewer, Woodbridge, 1999, 24. An overview of Hildegard's understanding of the relationship between the cosmos and microcosm is given in Flanagan, S., *Hildegard of Bingen: A Visionary Life*, Routledge, London and New York, 1990, 141–57.

23 Hildegard, *op. cit.*, 29.

24 Hildegard, *op. cit.*, 36.

25 Wolter OFM, A.B., and O'Neill OFM, B., *John Duns Scotus, Mary's Architect*, Franciscan Press, Quincy, Illinois, 1993, 51–4.

26 Rahner, K., 'The Immaculate Conception', in *Theological Investigations* Vol. 1 (trans. C. Ernst, Darton, Longman & Todd, London, 1974, 201–13.

27 Rahner, *op. cit.*, is a good example of this.

28 Saint John Eudes, *The Admirable Heart of Mary* (trans. C. de Targiani and R. Hauser), P.J. Kennedy and Sons, New York, 1948.

29 Eudes, *op. cit.*, 19.

30 Eudes, *op. cit.*, 38.

31 Eudes, *op. cit.*, 14.

32 Eudes, *op. cit.*, 19–20.

33 Eudes, *op. cit.*, 24.

34 Eudes, *op. cit.*, 38.

35 Eudes, *op. cit.*, 43

36 Warner, M., *Alone of All Her Sex: The Myth and the Cult of the Virgin Mary*, Quartet Books, London, 1978, 265–7; Boss, S. J., 'Guardians of the Way', in Warner, M., (ed.) *Say Yes to God: Mary and the Revealing of the Word Made Flesh*, Tufton Books, London, 1999, 95–122 at 107–9.

37 Eudes, *op. cit.*, 55.

38 Eudes, *op. cit.*, 27.

39 Kelly, J.N.D., *Early Christian Doctrines*, A & C Black, London, 1977, 297.

40 Le Breton, D., *Anthropologie du Corps et Modernité*, Quadrige/Presses Universitaires de France, Paris, 1990.

41 Le Breton, *op. cit.*, 22–8.

42 For a detailed and intelligent discussion of European tales of metamorphosis, see Walker-Bynum, C., *Metamorphosis and Identity*, Zone Books, New York, 2001.

43 Le Breton, *op. cit.*, 52. Le Breton cites Pouchelle, M.-C., *Corps et Chirurgie à l'Apogée du Moyen Age*, Flammarion, Paris, 1983, 137.

44 *The Quest of the Holy Grail* (trans. P.M. Matarasso), Penguin, Harmondsworth, 1969.

45 D'Arcy, A.M., *Wisdom and the Grail: The Image of the Vessel in the 'Queste Del Saint Graal' and Malory's 'Tale of Sankgreal'*, Four Courts Press, Dublin, 2000, 80–1, n.36.

46 Le Breton, *op. cit.*, 46.

47 Le Breton, *op. cit.*, 54.

3

The All-Holy One

The Virgin's sanctity

That Mary is the Mother of God makes her unique amongst human beings, as does the fact that she is both a virgin and a mother. And these doctrines are closely connected to one another. Early Christian writers say the fact that Mary is a mother shows that Christ is truly human, since he is born of a human mother, whilst the fact that she remains a virgin is a sign that he is truly divine, since this is a miracle that could be accomplished only by God. Not surprisingly, then, ancient tradition maintains that Mary's life was always marked out in ways that indicated her special status. The earliest full account of Mary's early life is given in a work that is usually known as the *Protevangelium of James* – 'protevengelium' meaning 'that which comes before the gospel', because it recounts the life of Mary from before the earliest time recorded in the New Testament Gospels, whilst the designation 'of James' signifies the book's spurious claim to have been written by St James the Less.[1] Most of this work seems to have been written during the second century, and many of the events that it records have entered into the ordinary teaching of the Catholic and Orthodox churches, being retold down the centuries, and taking the form of feast days, popular traditions and works of art. In the narrative of the *Protevangelium*, Mary's exceptional status, and that of her son, is shown by the occurrence of miracles, whilst her special suitability for this status is shown by her exceptional consecration to the Lord. Briefly, the story runs as follows.

Anna and Joachim were a righteous Jewish couple who longed to have children. Their childlessness was a cause for mockery from their neighbours, since it showed they had not received the Lord's blessing. So Anna sang a lament, in which she compared herself to other creatures on earth – birds, beasts and water – bemoaning the fact that these were all fruitful, and she alone was barren. Then an angel of the Lord appeared to her and let her know that the Lord had heard her prayer and that she would conceive and bear a child. Anna said that if this did indeed come to pass, then

Figure 2. Our Lady of Boulogne

she would offer the child to the service of the Lord all the days of its life. And Joachim, tending his flocks, likewise received an angelic visitation, giving him the same news; so he went to find his wife, who flung her arms around his neck with joy, and the couple returned home together. After this, as the angel had said, they conceived a child.

This account of a conception to an apparently barren couple, heralded by an angelic announcement, clearly follows biblical precedents – Sarah's conception of Isaac (Genesis 18.1–15; 21.17), Hannah's of Samuel (1 Samuel 1.1–20), and Elizabeth's of John the Baptist (Luke 1.5–24; 2.57–66). The consecration to the Lord's service seems to echo the dedication of Samuel to the Temple (1 Samuel 1.21–28).

When the child was born, it was a girl, and they called her Mary. Mary took her first steps at six months old, and after this, Anna 'made a sanctuary in her bedroom and did not permit anything common or unclean to pass through it'. The girl who is dedicated to the Lord is thus set apart from mundane things.

This 'sanctuary of her bedroom' shelters little Mary until she is three years old, when she is taken to the much greater sanctuary of the Lord's Temple, accompanied by 'the undefiled daughters of the Hebrews', each one bearing a torch so that Mary will not be tempted to look back and desire anything other than the Temple of the Lord. On arriving at the Temple, Mary is received by the priest, who blesses and praises her, and places her on the third step of the altar, where she dances, 'and the whole house of Israel loved her'. From then on, Mary lives in the Temple, where she receives food from the hand of an angel. The Temple, which is the dwelling place of the unseen God, seems itself to be a type of Mary, who is to become the dwelling place of God incarnate.

At the age of twelve, the priests decide that she cannot remain in the Temple for much longer, lest she 'defile' it. They are evidently anxious about menstrual pollution, and the narrator may intend a certain irony here. For surely the woman who is so sacred that she is to bear God in her own body cannot present a threat of ritual impurity to the building whose holiness will be surpassed through her own childbearing? The priests, however, must observe the Law as it stands. So the high priest, Zacharias, goes into the Holy of Holies to seek the Lord's guidance. There, an angel appears to him and tells him to assemble the widowers of the people, saying that Mary should become the wife of whichever of them is indicated by a sign from the Lord. When the men are assembled, Joseph is among them, an old man. Each man is given a rod, and out of Joseph's rod there flies a dove which lands upon his head. We might again wonder whether there is not an ironic touch to this narrative. The motif of a bird flying from a man's staff seems a rather obvious symbol of male sexuality, but we shall go on to read that Mary does not have sexual intercourse with Joseph. In the Gospels, a dove signifies the Holy Spirit when it descends upon Jesus at his baptism, so it may be intended to indicate only that Joseph is the chosen one of God.

After the betrothal, Mary goes to live in Joseph's house while he is away at his work as a builder. While Joseph is away, the priests decide to have a new veil made for the Temple. They call together seven virgins of the tribe of David, and give them the various threads to spin. Mary is one of these virgins, and she is given the purple and the scarlet. She goes home and spins the scarlet. After this comes the Annunciation, which is slightly different from the narrative given in Luke's Gospel.

Mary takes a pitcher and goes to draw water. While she is doing this, she hears a voice saying, 'Hail, highly favoured one, the Lord is with you, you are blessed among women.'[2] Trembling, Mary goes into her house, puts down the pitcher and starts spinning the purple thread. Then an angel appears to her and announces that she will conceive by the Word of 'the Lord of all things'. Mary questions the angel, as a result of which it emerges that she will not 'bear as every woman bears', because 'the power of the Lord' will overshadow her. Mary then takes the completed purple and scarlet to the priest.

Mary's spinning of the thread for the veil of the Temple must be of symbolic importance. There is surely a comparison here between the Temple, which is the dwelling place of God under the earlier dispensation that was given to the Jewish people, and Mary, who, in the new dispensation, is the dwelling place of God incarnate. The veil was that which hid the Holy of Holies from human sight, as Mary's body will be the veil for God as he gestates in her womb. Yet Mary's body will also be the instrument of the revelation of God in the form of a creature, and thus will reveal what the Temple veil hides.

As in Luke's Gospel, the *Protevangelium* recounts that Mary visits her cousin Elizabeth. Subsequently, Joseph discovers that Mary is pregnant, and, as in Matthew's Gospel, has a dream in which an angel appears in order to reassure him of the sacred character of her conception. Both Mary and Joseph are then subjected to a trial by ordeal to see whether the couple have broken their sacred trust by having had sexual intercourse. They are found innocent.

The narrative of the birth of Christ in a cave is perhaps the most striking part of the *Protevangelium*, since it tells of the natural world – human beings, animals and water – standing still at the moment of the birth, of the cave being overshadowed by a bright cloud, followed by its being filled with a great light, and of a birth that is so miraculous that Mary's body afterwards is unchanged from its virginal state. The midwife testifies to this, but another woman, Salome, does not believe the midwife's word, and so places her finger into Mary's body to test her condition. As she does this, her hand withers, consumed by fire. The hand is healed when Salome touches the child after repenting of her unbelief.

As in Matthew, the *Protevangelium* tells of the visit of the Magi, and of their innocently informing King Herod of the birth of 'the king of the Jews'. To prevent himself from being usurped, Herod commands the massacre of all infants under two years old. The final episodes of the book tell of Herod's attempt to find Jesus and kill him, and of the miraculous rescuing of Elizabeth and John the Baptist from Herod's soldiers, when the mother and child are hidden in a mountain. The child's father, however, is not so fortunate, and he is murdered because Herod believes that it is Zacharias' son who is to be the new king over Israel, and Zacharias refuses to say where the boy is hidden.

Part of the theological intention behind the *Protevangelium* is certainly to demonstrate the divinity of Christ. This is part of what is shown, for example, in Mary's miraculous parturition, and in the correspondence that is implicitly drawn between Mary and the Temple. However, most commentators think that the book also bears witness to a very early devotion to Mary herself within the Christian church. The account of Mary's being set apart from the mundane world all through her childhood signifies her sacred status,[3] as does her virginal childbearing and the ferocious consequences that befall the woman who doubts her physical integrity. One characteristic of things that are sacred is that when they are treated with appropriate reverence, they bestow blessing, but that when they are treated disrespectfully, they impart misfortune. The withering of Salome's hand is a clear indicator of the sanctity of Mary's virginal body.

This property – of bringing blessing when treated respectfully and causing harm when dishonoured – is an endowment of the natural world as well. When treated with reverence it may yield blessings, but when abused, it generates destruction. We might wonder whether it is not from nature that humanity first learnt the meaning of holiness.

The nature of the sacred

Sociologists and anthropologists have debated hotly the notion of the 'sacred', or the 'holy', that is, what it is that constitutes an object as sacred or signifies its sanctity. However, I am going to draw on one of the earliest anthropological presentations of the 'sacred', that of Emile Durkheim,[4] because it brings attention to a feature of sacred objects and actions that is relevant to a consideration of the holiness of the Virgin Mary.

The French composer Pierre Boulez has commented that what distinguishes the modern approach to the world from those that have gone before is its refusal to allow any 'sanctuaries'. That is to say, there is no forbidden territory. In music, Boulez's own expertise, it was once the case that, for example, only certain harmonic progressions were permitted. These changed over time, but there were always musical intervals that were forbidden to the composer. In the nineteenth and twentieth centuries, by contrast, every possible kind of harmony and melodic progression has become open to experimentation.

Likewise, in the area of the natural sciences, many features of the natural world were once regarded as out of bounds to human intervention, or could be exploited or investigated only under the most rigorous controls. Since the Scientific Revolution of the seventeenth century, however, ever increasingly large areas of the material world have come under human scrutiny, and the sciences in themselves lay down no restrictions upon the possible scope of their own activities.[5]

This notion of the sacred as that which is forbidden and kept apart from everyday activity is central to Durkheim's understanding of the phenomenon. He argues that, in human societies in general, the sacred and the profane are categories that are utterly opposed to one another. One may pass from one to the other, but the two are quite distinct, as is exemplified in the ideal of monasticism, whereby a man or woman leaves the ordinary, profane world in order to move into an enclosed space that is sacred and set apart from the mundane. Ritual objects similarly have to be treated separately from other things. In a Catholic church, vessels and linen that have been used for communion, that is, which have come into contact with the body and blood of Christ under the form of the bread and wine of the Eucharist, are supposed to be washed in water that runs into earth – a natural element – and not get mixed up with profane cloths and vessels. This kind of distinction between the sacred and the profane clearly underpins much of the narrative of the *Protevangelium*. Mary as the Godbearer is a sacred being, as the Temple as God's dwelling is a sacred building, and is thus set apart from mundane things.

People working for nature conservation have used a variety of different arguments to support the preservation of particular wildlife sites and endangered species: scientific importance and aesthetic value have both been pressed into service to these ends. Yet underlying these explicitly stated concerns is an intuition that nature should be treated with reverence – that certain things should be protected, as Mary was protected, because they are holy.

The specific danger from which holy things must be protected – the desecration that rebounds on those who perpetrate it – is called *pollution*. Pollution is primarily a ritual concept, applied to the contamination of nature by analogy: or perhaps not by analogy, but because the profanation of earth, air and water is precisely the pollution of the sacred.

Growth and form

The sacred power of nature is founded in the creative activity of God its Maker, and a strong sense of Mary's association with this power is expressed in these verses of a poem by Gerard Manley Hopkins:

> flesh and fleece, fur and feather,
> Grass and greenworld all together:
> Starry-eyed and strawberry-breasted
> Throstle above her nested
>
> Cluster of bugle blue eggs thin
> Forms and warms the life within;
> And bird and blossom swell
> In sod or sheath or shell.
>
> All things rising, all things sizing
> Mary sees, sympathising
> With that world of good,
> Nature's motherhood.[6]

Amongst the English Jesuit community at Stonyhurst College in Lancashire, it used to be the custom for community members to write poems in honour of the Virgin Mary during the month of May, and to display them in 'Our Lady's Gallery'. The verses quoted above are taken from the poem 'The May Magnificat', which Hopkins wrote as a May offering of this kind while he was living at Stonyhurst in the 1880s. None of the Virgin's major feast days falls in May, but, as we have already seen, the whole month is traditionally dedicated to her. Hopkins' poem points out that there is nothing contrived or artificial about this, for Christ is the author of life itself, so that in the paradox of Chrsitian doctrine, Mary, as the mother of Christ, is the mother of all new life, and thus of the growing and greening of springtime. It will be clear by now that the association of Mary with the natural world is a recurrent motif in Christian devotion to her, and perhaps for this reason is rarely commented upon: it is taken for granted. But it deserves explicit attention, both because it is tied to important theological truths about the relationship between God and creation, and because consideration of these truths provides Christian insight into the nature of our current ecological crisis and points to the spiritual re-orientation that we need to undertake if we are to address this crisis properly. To be properly concerned with Mary as she is known in doctrine and devotion, is to be equally concerned with the relationship between God and creation, and the human responsibilities which follow from that.

A striking example of the association that Christians have made between Mary and the material world is provided by a seventeenth-century account of the shrine of Our Lady of Núria, in the Catalan Pyrenees. Núria is a remote mountain valley, traditionally used by herdsmen for grazing their flocks in the high meadows during the summer months of July to September. It is also the home of the miracle-working statue of Our Lady of Nuria, and hence is a place of pilgrimage.

In 1666, a book was published which, although entitled *History and Miracles of the Holy Image of Our Lady of Núria*,[7] begins with a fairly detailed description of the physical geography and natural history of the valley. The author makes observations concerning the mountains, springs, flora and fauna of the area. Parts of the description have something of the picturesque about them, as when we are told that at Núria the pilgrim will find scented pinks and many varieties of rose, and that Mary's shrine is surrounded by lilies: 'although no human hand cultivates them, yet the divine Author of all things spreads them out in profusion to serve as an embellishment for the resting-place of the Queen of the universe!'[8] Yet this does not distract the author's attention from the fact that ice and snow make the place inaccessible and uninhabitable in winter, and that even in the summer: 'The paths which lead to the hermitage are so bad that only the desire to venerate the miraculous image of the Queen of Angels can give you the courage necessary to confront the difficulties.'[9] Not surprisingly, when travellers come within sight of the chapel, many cry with joy, and some fall to their knees and kiss the holy ground.[10] Thus, the reader is implicitly told, the world of physical nature may abound with objects of delight, but also with a harshness that can overwhelm human life and health.

In traditional Christian philosophy, evil is something that resides not only in those human actions that Christians describe as 'sinful', but also in the very fabric of the universe, being manifest in the suffering and death, and perhaps even the transience, that pervade the natural order. According to Christian mythology, Satan – a fallen angel who was jealous of humanity and had set himself in opposition to God – tempted the first man and woman, Adam and Eve, to disobey their maker. They gave way to the temptation, and thus it was humanity who introduced wickedness into the world; but its bad effects harm the rest of creation in one way or another. Yet the world was made by God in a state of goodness, and retains that fundamental goodness in spite of the ubiquitous influence of evil. Moreover, God intends that all evil will finally be destroyed when creation is brought to its fulfilment. The Blessed Virgin Mary embodies the goodness of God's original creation, and is the beginning and sign of its future perfection. She is the opponent whom Satan most fears. For this reason, Mary is hailed as the 'refuge of sinners': she offers the hope of freedom from bondage to sin. Since she also offers the hope of freedom from suffering in general, she has been called upon to assist men and women in every possible extremity, from the dangers of childbirth to those of the battlefield. Likewise, her image has been perceived in many aspects of non-human nature, as though the splendour in which creation was made and the glory for which it is destined does not cease to shine forth in the present order of things.

Throughout Europe, a large number of flowers has traditionally been associated with Mary. In England, marigold (Mary's gold), lady's bedstraw (Our Lady's bedstraw), lady's bower (clematis), and lady's mantle are just a few. Yet she has been seen not only in the delicacy of wild flowers, but also in the vastness of the night sky. In 1871, in the village of Pontmain, in Normandy, a little boy went out in the darkness of a clear January evening, and looking up into the Milky Way, saw the image of the Virgin Mary, her mantle covered with stars. Now this was at a time when the Prussian army was advancing through northern France, and terrified villagers were praying for deliverance from the threat of war or military defeat. Mary-in-the-stars offered the little boy a large red cross, and said, 'My Son allows himself to be moved.' Ten days later, a full armistice was signed and peace returned to the country.[11]

Cardigan, Núria and Pontmain all display a characteristic feature of devotion to Mary, that is, the custom of associating her with quite particular places, usually because of some sacred aspect of the natural world. If we look again to France, we find that at the famous shrine of Lourdes there is a healing spring,[12] whilst at the more ancient shrine of Our Lady of Rocamadour, a hollow in the rock is the dwelling-place of the miraculous statue of the Virgin.[13] Boulogne is situated by the sea over which, according to legend, Mary miraculously sailed in the year 633, to establish a cliff-top shrine which commands the English Channel for miles around (Figure 2).[14] And throughout the world, Mary takes the name of the place where she is enshrined. She is Our Lady of Czestochowa (in Poland), Our Lady of Walsingham (in England), or Our Lady of Guadalupe (in both Spain and Mexico). As the poet David Jones observed, 'She's a rare one for locality.' We too must attend to locality, for if we do not reverence God's creatures in their particular forms in their particular places, then we do not see God at work in creation at all.

To those who are attentive, the Virgin's presence in nature has been manifested in modern Britain, just as it was in the Middle Ages and as it has been more recently in continental Europe. At a conference in Oxford in 2000, the Catholic writer Stratford Caldecott presented a paper on the subject of Marian influences in the novels of J.R.R. Tolkien. Caldecott began by describing an experience of his own, in which, during a coach journey to an English Marian shrine, he had had an intense awareness of the Virgin Mary's pervasive presence in the folds of the hills through which he was travelling. Tolkien's own evocations of landscape are one of the things that draw many readers to his work – a landscape evidently based on the countryside of southern Britain. It seems probable, however, that most readers of *The Lord of the Rings* are not aware of a comment that the author, a devout Catholic, made in a letter to the Jesuit (now eminent Syriac scholar) Robert Murray, in 1953, the year of the book's publication:

> I think I know exactly what you mean by the order of Grace, and of course by your references to Our Lady, upon which all my own small perception of beauty both in majesty and simplicity is founded.[15]

Commenting upon the religious underpinnings of Tolkien's work, Stratford Caldecott quotes this sentence, drawing attention to the reference to the Virgin, and observes:

> Tolkien's novel is permeated with beauty, from the natural beauties of landscape and forest, mountains and streams, to the moral beauty of heroism and integrity, friendship and honesty.[16]

Tolkien detested modern technology, because of its tendency to destroy life and to treat people as though they too were machines. His opposition to technology finds expression in *The Lord of the Rings*, where machines are possessed and enjoyed only by the evil characters, such as Orcs.[17] And indeed, if the whole of creation in some way has a Marian character, then we must ask what moral consequences follow from this – which is to say (in part, at least), what sort of technology may we legitimately devise and use in such a sacred world?

Notes

1 'The Protevangelium of James', in Elliott, J. K. (ed.), *The Apocryphal New Testament: A Collection of Apocryphal Christian literature in an English Translation*, Clarendon Press, Oxford, 1993, 48–67.

2 This greeting may be read as an amalgam of Luke 1.28 and 42, and constitutes the beginning of the Western church's most popular prayer to Mary, the Hail Mary, a fact which makes one wonder whether the short form of this prayer might not be very ancient.

3 See the analysis of the *Protevangelium* in Foskett, M.F., *A Virgin Conceived: Mary and Classical Representations of Virginity*, Indiana University Press, Bloomington, Indiana, 2002.

4 Durkheim, E., *The Elementary Forms of the Religious Life* (trans. J. Ward Swain), George Allen & Unwin, London, 1915, 38–41. I do not mean to imply that I accept Durkheim's interpretation of the sacred in any respect other than that which I discuss here.

5 A brief survey of the literature concerning these changes is given in Boss, S.J., *Empress and Handmaid: On Nature and Gender in the Cult of the Virgin Mary*, Cassell, London, 2000, 94–8.

6 Hopkins, G.M., 'The May Magnificat', in *Poems and Prose* (selected by W.H. Gardner), Penguin, Harmondsworth, 1953, 37–9.

7 Duque i Vergés, F.M.A. del, *Historia y Miracles de la Sagrad Imatge de Nostra Senyora de Nuria* [facsimile reproduction of edition of 1666], Editorial Alta Fulla, Barcelona, 2000; *Histoire de l'Ermitage de Notre-Dame de Nuria et des Principaux Miracles qui s'y sont opérés* [facsimile reproduction of French translation of 1867], Centre d'Estudis Comarcals del Ripollès, Ripoll, 1998.

8 Duque i Vergés, F.M.A. del, *op. cit.*, 14.

9 Duque i Vergés, F.M.A. del, *op. cit.*, 9–10.

10 Duque i Vergés, F.M.A. del, *op. cit.*, 11.

11 Laurentin, R. and Durand, A., *Pontmain: Histoire authentique. 1: Un signe dans le ciel*, Apostolat des Editions / Lethielleux, Paris, 1970, 13–52.

12 There are very many accounts of the shrine at Lourdes. The best recent one is Harris, R., *Lourdes: Body and Spirit in the Secular Age*, Penguin, Harmondsworth, 1999.

13 Boss, S.J., 'Guardians of the Way', in Warner, M., *Say Yes to God: Mary and the Revealing of the Word Made Flesh*, Tufton Press, London, 1999, 99–122.

14 Lejeune, F., *Notre-Dame de Boulogne* (series 'Les Grands Pèlerinages de France'), Letouzey et Ané, Paris, 1925, 6–9.

15 From Letter 142 of Tolkien's *Letters* (Allen & Unwin, London, 1981), 142. Cited in Caldecott, S., 'The Lord and Lady of the Rings: The hidden presence of Tolkien's Catholicism in *The Lord of the Rings*', in *Touchstone*, special issue. *J.R.R. Tolkien and the Christian Imagination*, The Fellowship of St. James, Chicago, 2002.

16 Caldecott, S., *op. cit.*

17 Veldman, M., *Fantasy, the Bomb and the Greening of Britain: Romantic Protest, 1945–1980*, Cambridge University Press, Cambridge, 1994, 80–90.

4
Heaven on Earth

Gestation

The Conceiving

Now
You are in the ark of my blood
in the river of my bones
in the woodland of my muscles
in the ligaments of my hair
in the wit of my hands
in the smear of my shadow
in the armada of my brain
under the stars of my skull
in the arms of my womb
Now you are here
you worker in the gold of flesh[1]

This remarkable poem by Penelope Shuttle plays with the exchange of images ('the ark of my blood' / 'the river of my bones'; 'the woodland of my muscles' / 'the ligaments of my hair') to create a sense of the union of the newly conceived child with its mother, a union of such a kind that one cannot tell where the one begins and the other ends, or indeed, what belongs to human, and what to non-human, nature ('the woodland of my muscles' / 'the stars of my skull'). In the Incarnation of the Word of God in Mary's womb, this union occurs not only between the mother and her child, but at the same time between God and creation. So to a Christian, Shuttle's muddling of imagery might suggest the paradoxical language that is the only possible language for speaking of the Incarnation. God, who is without beginning, is born of a woman. God, who has need of nothing, is nourished by his mother's milk. As it says in the fifteenth-century carol:

There is no rose of such virtue
As is the rose that bear Jesu. *Allelulia.*
For in that rose containèd was
Heaven and earth in little space. *Res Miranda.*

Time and eternity, space and infinity, motherhood and virginity, are incomprehensibly united in the Virgin's body.

Penelope Shuttle's poem speaks of how in even an ordinary pregnancy two people exist as it were in one substance. In this chapter, we shall consider how it may be that, in the case of Mary and Christ, consubstantiality continues in some measure beyond birth, through life, through death, and into heavenly glory. Christ is always a worker in the gold of a portion of Mary's flesh; and Mary's flesh is always present in that work of alchemical transmutation whereby God unites the things of earth to the things of heaven in our incarnate Lord, and thus brings all things to fulfilment.

Sandra Steingraber is an ecologist who, in her book *Having Faith*, describes her experience of becoming a mother, interspersing the account of her own pregnancy with professional insights into the processes of gestation. In doing this, she gives the reader a sense not only of the union of mother and child, but also of the union of both with the complex environment in which they survive. Citing the work of the medical historian Ann Dally, Steingraber recounts how, in antiquity and the middle ages, it was assumed that the pregnant mother and her child existed as a single unit: it was believed that the blood in the mother's body fed that of the foetus, so that the two existed as one being. In the early modern period, however, supposed experts began to adopt the view that the foetus developed in a sac that quite separated it from its mother. In particular, it was supposed that the placental barrier protected the developing infant from the effects of toxic chemicals. The foetus was already an idealized 'individual' within the increasingly dominant culture of bourgeois individualism. This belief continued so doggedly that, well into the twentieth century, many physicians did not identify that poisons present in the pregnant mother could be transmitted from her to the foetus, and this belief delayed the identification of the harmful effects of both rubella and thalidomide upon the developing child. Many infant deformities were thus caused by the refusal to acknowledge the continuity of a mother with her unborn infant. It was not until the 1950s that belief in the infant's protected environment finally began to be put to rest.[2]

Nowadays, the tendency to regard the foetus as clearly individuated from its mother may be more characteristic of men than of women. But in the past, it seems that both men and women recognized not only the union of mother and unborn child, but, as we have already seen, a certain union of all things in creation. With the culture of individualism, by contrast, there arose not only a refusal to recognize the solidarity of human beings with other creatures, but even the solidarity of the maternal body with its immanent offspring.

In this chapter, we shall try to recover a sense of the continuity of things with one another, extending as far as the union of heaven and earth, by examining the mariology of the great sixteenth-century theologian Francisco Suárez (1548–1617), a mariology which focuses specifically on the physical relationship between mother and child.

Suárez's mariology

In his principle work of Marian theology,[3] Suárez states at the outset that everything which he will say of the Virgin rests on the divine motherhood, its dignity [*dignitas*], and the Virgin's predestination to it.[4] He uses the Scriptures and Church Fathers to argue the case that Mary is truly the Mother of God, and then adds 'a conjecture, or congruence', as follows:

> For doubtless God wished to communicate himself to people by all kinds of means, and, so to say, to contract with them all kinds of kinship, by blood and by affinity, that tend towards perfection; yet one kind [of kinship], and one which is exceedingly perfect, exists that God may not so much be man but even the son of man, and that some created human person may be joined together with God [*conjuncta Deo*], in so far as is possible with regard to a person. Whence indeed it is accomplished that not only human nature in Christ, but also a created person in the Virgin, will have been exalted above all the choirs of angels.[5]

Thus, Mary's being the Mother of God is not merely an implicit adjunct to the Incarnation, but is an end in itself, because it is the one relationship in which a human person is joined to God in the most complete manner possible. At first glance, one might think that this view is mistaken, since it is the humanity of Christ, not of Mary, that is joined to God most perfectly. But although in Christ the human and divine natures are perfectly united, in the technical formulation of Christian doctrine, Christ's *person* is divine and not human.

When the ecumenical church Council of Chalcedon met in 451, the term

'Person' had been employed for many decades to designate a member of the Blessed Trinity; and in the case of Christ, Chalcedon ruled that the second Person – the eternal Word – was the principle uniting the divine and human natures. This was not seen as compromising Christ's full humanity. The Christological definition of Chalcedon, which is followed by the Catholic, major Protestant, and Eastern Orthodox churches, includes the statement that Christ is 'one person in two natures'. The natures are human and divine, but the person, being the second Person of the Trinity, is only divine. So Suárez's point about Mary's being joined to God makes it clear that even a creature who is not, by nature, divine – who is not uncreated, eternal and infinite – has the capacity for the most intimate possible union with the Blessed Trinity.

In Suárez's thought, Mary's being uniquely joined to God corresponds to, and is a consequence of, a similarly unique closeness that exists between her and Christ in the Incarnation. For in the human flesh which he shares with his mother, Christ is bound to her in an altogether singular way. Suárez quotes St Peter Damian as saying, 'Whilst God may be present in other things in three ways, in the Virgin he was present in a fourth, special way, namely, by identity, because he is the same as that which she is.'[6] Suárez also observes that 'some substance of her virginal body, from which Christ's body was [taken] and first formed, and afterwards grew, for as long as it was nourished by his mother's blood or milk, would be hypostatically united to the Word of God'.[7] Moreover, since Augustine claims that the flesh of Christ, which is transformed by the glory of the Resurrection, nevertheless remains the same flesh that was taken from Mary, Suárez thinks that, as the human Christ matured, the substance of flesh which he originally assumed from the Virgin was never entirely lost, but was always conserved, united to the Word of God.[8] This certainly seems to be a curious doctrine, but Suárez's insistence on the continuing union of Mary's flesh with the Word of God points almost graphically to the capacity of even our blood and our guts to be bound to and transformed by the divine presence.

Now, although Suárez's teaching on this point is somewhat unusual, Suárez himself is a figure of such outstanding importance in European intellectual history, including Catholic theology, that his teaching cannot be dismissed out of hand as merely quirky. Throughout the Tridentine era (that is, the period between the Council of Trent [1545–63] and the Second Vatican Council [1962–65]), the name of Francisco Suárez was commonplace in Catholic educational institutions and beyond. He was born in Granada in 1548 and joined the Society of Jesus (the Jesuits) at the age of sixteen.

He then spent the rest of his life in Jesuit academic institutions, including Rome – where he worked out much of his thinking on the Virgin Mary – and Coimbra (Portugal), where he spent the longest period of time, and where he died in 1617. So his work took place in the decades immediately following the Council of Trent.[9] Suárez was a man of many parts: most famously, perhaps, he was an extremely important legal theorist. He is often thought of as the founder of international law; and the Hispanic countries of the world still have legal systems that draw heavily on Suárezian principles. He was also an important philosopher: his moral theology and theory of canon law were employed in Catholic ethical thinking until very recently, and his *Metaphysics* was a standard work in European universities, both Catholic and Protestant, for the better part of two centuries.[10]

Suárez's view of the human condition is favourable and hopeful. In the Foreword to his major work on law, *De Legibus*, he asks why a theologian should be concerned with laws. In reply, he argues that the theologian is concerned with God as, amongst other things, 'the final end to which rational creatures are striving', and in whom is their ultimate happiness; and the function of legal systems is to help those creatures attain their end in God, who is also himself the legislator.[11] So the purpose of law is not merely the correction of sinfulness, but primarily, the generation of righteousness and the attainment of heaven. Suárez's ethical theory and his understanding of God's general dealings with humanity assume that God has ordered the world in such a way that it is always within the grasp of a man or woman to increase in merit and come nearer to perfection. Suárez's teaching on the Blessed Virgin Mary presents her as the one who reaches humanity's final destination by following the most perfect path that is possible for a human being.

Amongst his theological writings, Suárez's longest text on the Virgin Mary, composed mainly in the 1580s, is generally reckoned to be the first of its kind. That is to say, it is the first systematic treatment of Marian doctrine as a whole. Earlier authors had dealt with particular Marian questions, such as those concerning the Immaculate Conception; but Suárez organized the various topics of Marian doctrine into a coherent whole, each part being linked to the others by means of neo-scholastic argument, and the entire treatise being set within the wider body of Christian theology.

As we have seen, Suárez's treatment of Marian doctrine begins by establishing that she is the Mother of God, and everything else that he says about her follows from this office, from the honour intrinsic to it, and from the Virgin's predestination to it. Suárez establishes the truth of the divine

motherhood (i.e., that Mary is the Mother of God) by arguing from the
Scriptures – in which Mary is the mother of Christ, who is God – and then
from the teaching of the ecumenical Council of Ephesus (AD 431). Having
established the truth of the divine motherhood – on the basis of Scripture,
the authority of a Church Council and rational argument – Suárez then has
a foundation on which to construct other lines of argument about Mary.
For example, he argues that God bestowed upon her an exceptional degree
of grace from the moment of her conception. And his main argument for
this is related directly to the divine motherhood. This is how the argument
goes. As a general principle – apart from his mariology – Suárez argues
that God gives us the grace that is necessary for us to perform the task to
which God calls us: if God requires me to visit the sick, or if God requires
me to die as a martyr, or whatever it may be, God will give me the grace
sufficient to that task. Now, in Mary's case, she was called to be the Mother
of God. That, according to Suárez, is the greatest task that any simple
human being (i.e., one who is not God incarnate) ever has been or could be
called upon to perform. Accordingly, the grace that Mary received, being
commensurate with the task and the office [Latin: *dignitas*] to which she
was called, was the greatest that anyone has ever received.[12]

Moreover, following the teaching of John Duns Scotus, as we have seen
above, the incarnation of the Word of God in Christ was predestined from
before the foundation of the world, and not only as a response to human
sinfulness;[13] and since the Incarnation consisted in part, at least, in Mary
giving Christ his humanity – in her being the Mother of God – Mary's
divine motherhood must have been predestined in the same act by which
God predestined the Incarnation.[14] That means that there was no point at
which Mary was not going to be the Mother of God.[15] So from the moment
of Mary's conception, God called her to the divine motherhood. Since her
whole life would have been ordered to this supreme dignity, according to
Suárez, we can be sure that God will have bestowed upon Mary an exceptional degree of grace from the very first moment of her life.[16]

The divine motherhood, and Mary's predestination to it, is the reason
for all the other blessings that she receives, and the doctrine that she is the
mother of God informs everything else that systematic theology can say about
her. The union of creature and Creator in the Incarnation is the culmination
of the single providence of God working throughout the universe, and may
perhaps be seen as emblematic of it. In this scheme for the glorification of
the universe, Mary constitutes the perfection of the human condition; but
since the human condition encapsulates the creation, she is at the same time

the perfection of all the world, her flesh being that which is united to God in Christ. This perfection means bearing a sacred and humble responsibility towards other creatures; and in Mary's relationship with her son, by which God and creation are united, we see the presence of heaven on earth, and thus the fulfilment of humanity's right relationship with both God and creation.

Suárez's picture of Mary as the human person most closely joined to God follows a long tradition of describing the Incarnation in terms of a movement of mirroring: the Word 'descends' into flesh so that those who are made of flesh may 'ascend' to be with God in glory. Mary, whose flesh was the particular flesh assumed by the Word, is the principal example of human ascent to heaven mirroring the divine descent to earth.[17] For Suárez, Mary's glorification is articulated in particularly strong language, thereby emphasizing the creature's potential to reflect and be united to divinity.

If we return now to consider the motif of Mary's flesh being always present in the body of Christ, I suggest that this too is a teaching that is concerned with the rendering of earth as a counterpart to heaven. The doctrine of shared flesh and consequent identity between human mother and human-divine Son, lasting into the condition of glorification, indicates how great is the capacity of the material creation to be glorified and joined together with God. In Mary, the physical creation participates in the glory shared by the angels and saints in God's immediate presence. As God comes to earth, the earthly is joined to God, and earth is cast in the image of heaven.

The likeness of the Trinity

'Thy will be done on Earth as it is in Heaven.' These words are repeated over and over again by Christians as they address God in the prayer that the Lord himself gave to his disciples, and the attainment of heaven on earth is in more than one sense the end to which the Christian religion is directed. What, then, is the nature of heaven, and how can we most properly characterize the relationship between heaven and earth? The Christian faith is preached on earth and is concerned with this planet and the physical cosmos, yet since the goal of the Christian life is the attainment of heaven, the answer to this question is of vital importance. Is earth a place of exile for souls who must endure a few decades of unsatisfactory physical life here before they reach their true homeland in a spiritual heaven that they will enter after death? Or is heaven a spiritual state already attainable on earth to those who know how to find it? Is heaven a state of affairs that can be brought about by human endeavour, or is it something that God alone will accomplish when the world is entirely transformed at the end of time? Each of these views, and various combinations of them, has been held by one group of Christians or another at some point in history. One element that is constant, however, is the understanding of 'heaven' as the state in which all things are, and know themselves to be, in the immediate presence of God. It is the place or condition in which God's will is already done, and whose likeness is desired on earth. And since God was uniquely present in the earthly life of Jesus Christ, Jesus in some way gives human beings a glimpse of heaven – of what it is to be in the immediate presence of God. In Christ, who is God and man, heaven and earth are bound together.

Christian writers have sometimes referred to the womb or the body of the Virgin Mary as another 'heaven', since she was the physical abode of God incarnate during her pregnancy. Thus, writing of Our Lady's own conception in her mother's womb, the sixteenth-century poet Robert Southwell says, 'Earth breedes a Heaven / For God's new dwelling-place.'[18] The association between Mary and Heaven is both ancient and deep. For example, since the early middle ages she has been understood to be the 'Queen of Heaven', and is often seen as the surest helper for people on earth who are seeking the way to union with God. Yet we have already seen that the association between Mary and earth, or Mary and the cosmos, is similarly deep, which suggests that the universe already has some sort of heavenly character. It is as though, by looking at Mary, we may see both the heavenly state implicit in creation as it is now, and the heavenly glory that is creation's final destiny.

Now, since everything in creation exists in relation to other things – and, at the deepest level, participates in all other things – it is never appropriate to consider Mary alone, as though she were independent of others. So we shall go on to consider further the ways in which theology and devotion have presented the relationship between Mary and her son, Jesus Christ, as Godlike, or heavenly, and what the broader implications of this may be for our understanding of God's participation in the created world, and consequently for our human responsibilities towards it.

Near the beginning of the present chapter I cited the first stanza of a fifteenth-century carol:

There is no rose of such virtue
As is the rose which bare Jesu: *Alleluia*.
For in that rose contained was
Heaven and earth in little space: *Res miranda*.

This is a mystical poem, that is, it has a spiritual meaning that is both hidden behind and disclosed through a symbolic text. The 'rose' is evidently the Virgin Mary, since it is she in whom heaven and earth were contained when she was pregnant with Jesus, the Creator of the universe – truly a 'res miranda', a marvellous thing. A part of the song whose meaning is less clear, however, is the stanza which begins:

> By that rose we may well see
> There be one God in Persons three.

For how is it that the mother of Christ can reveal the truth of the Blessed Trinity? The poem implies that we come to know this truth through contemplating Christ's birth and the Incarnation, rather than through rational argument.

Another fifteenth-century carol, 'Make We Joy', gives slightly more of a clue as to how the mystery of Christ's birth reveals that of the Trinity. The song begins with the chorus:

> Make we joy now in this feast
> *In quo Christus natus est.*   [In which Christ is born.]

The first verse then begins:

> *A Patre unigenitus*   [Of the Father sole-begotten]
> Through a maiden is come to us.

Verses four and five conclude the carol thus:

> *Maria ventre concipit,*   [Mary conceived in her belly]
> The Holy Ghost was ay her with:
> In Bethlehem yborn he is,
> *Consors paterni luminis*:   [Consort of the Father's light:]

> *O lux beata, Trinitas!*   [O blessed light, Trinity!]
> He lay between an ox and ass,
> And by his mother, maiden free.
> *Gloria tibi, Domine!*   [Glory to you, Lord!]

One aspect of this poem is the parallel that is drawn between Christ being, on the one hand, 'begotten of the Father', and on the other hand, conceived and born of his mother Mary. This theme was very popular in the Christmas sermons of early Christian writers, and is often referred to as the 'double nativity'. It is concerned with the paradox by which God the Son, who is eternally begotten, or 'born', of God, the first Person of the Trinity, is at the same time the human son of Mary, conceived by her and born in Bethlehem. In 'Make We Joy', it is this dual character to Christ's sonship which means that the contemplation of Christ's nativity is the occasion for revelation of the Trinity. Mary conceived in her womb by the Holy Spirit, and the child that is born of this conception is the Son who is only-begotten of the Father, and of one substance with the Father. This, indeed, is the meaning of the reference to the Trinity as 'light': as a flame that is lit from another flame does not diminish, or in any other way alter, the flame that is its source, so the Son's generation from the Father, and the Holy Spirit's from the Father and the Son, do not bring about any change in those Persons (the Father and the Son) in whom the other Persons (the Son and the Spirit, respectively) have their origin.

Christ being the son of Mary, by the power of the Holy Spirit, reveals to the world Christ's eternal sonship of the divine Father. For Mary's motherhood is in effect the created counterpart to the fatherhood of the first Person of the Trinity. She is the human parent to the Son of whom God is the eternal parent, and the human mother's relationship to her son is the earthly image of the divine Father's relationship to that same Son. Moreover, as we know from the circumstances of Christ's conception (also referred to in the carol quoted above), this whole mystery is wrought by God the Holy Spirit. It is thus that 'by that rose we may well see, there be one God in Persons three'.

Now, taken on its own, Suárez's proposal that the flesh of Mary always remains in Christ's body may seem eccentric and even bizarre. But I suggest that its theological purpose is not only to show the capacity of the material world for union with God, but also to present the relationship between Christ and his earthly mother as a created counterpart to and reflection of the relationship that exists between Christ and God the Father in eternity. For if Christ and Mary share 'one flesh', then they have a substantial union which may be seen as an echo of the consubstantiality of the Persons of the Trinity.[19]

Suárez refers to the idea of the double nativity at the very beginning of his principal Marian writing, as part of his apologia for devoting so much space to questions concerning the Blessed Virgin. He writes:

There was indeed the greatest necessity that this matter [i.e., knowledge of the Godbearer] should be treated fully. For just as the eternal procession of Christ cannot be believed without faith in the eternal Father, so his generation in time, which had its beginning from a mother without a father, cannot be grasped without prior knowledge of the Godbearer.[20]

That this is Suárez's opening consideration suggests that it should be understood as colouring or guiding much of what follows, and so it seems quite justified to interpret his suggestion that the flesh of Mary remained always in Christ as implying a certain parallel between Christ's relationship with his human mother and his relationship with his eternal Father.[21]

The insight that, in Mary's relationship with Christ, heaven is reflected on earth, is of profound importance for Christian anthropology, the theology of creation and a Christian response to the present ecological crisis. The Muslim writer Seyyed Hossein Nasr has argued that we only have a proper understanding of the earth which we inhabit when we see it in relation to heaven. He contends that one of the reasons why humanity is now destroying the earth, the air, the water and the living things which all manifest God's wisdom, is that men and women have lost any belief in heaven and thus see the earth in the wrong perspective – as devoid of sanctity.[22] Furthermore, to see earth as an actual and potential reflection of heaven is to have a spiritual benchmark by which to judge human action in the here-and-now. Do we respect the heavenly character of the world in which we live? Suárez's doctrine of the consubstantiality of Christ and Mary implies that in the Incarnation and divine motherhood, things of earth become a counterpart to the divine, and hence that the earth possesses the capacity for glorification, and therefore the kind of sanctity that Nasr argues it is imperative for us to recognize.

Now in general, Christian theologians, including Suárez, have argued that an act of the will – a conscious decision or attitude – carries a moral weight that a purely physical action does not. For example, St Bernard of Clairvaux (1090–1153), in one of his homilies in praise of the Blessed Virgin Mary, enjoins his audience to take note of both her virginity and her humility. Mary's virginity is a physical state and her humility a condition of the soul. Bernard says that both these things are praiseworthy. But, he says, if you are a virgin and are *proud* of your virginity – if you boast about it – then it is of little moral worth. Furthermore, not everyone is called to be a virgin; but even people who are not virgins are called to be humble, and humility is a great virtue whatever one's physical state may be. So although the physical state of virginity is good, the moral state of humility takes precedence.[23]

If we follow this line of thought, then we might be inclined to say that Mary's moral consent to be the mother of Christ is of greater worth than her physical conception of God incarnate in her womb. She hears the word of God and keeps it, and surely that is what counts the most? But Suárez points out that in the case of Mary's conception of Christ, we are dealing with a matter that is of a completely different order from that which is at issue with other people under different circumstances. All God's saints 'hear the word of God and keep it', as Mary did. But Mary also conceived and gave birth to God incarnate, the saviour of the world, which the others did not. So her physical act of conceiving and bearing Christ is a unique, miraculous and indispensable element in God's redemption of the world, and as such, it cannot properly be compared to an ordinary moral assent to God's will. Ordinary obedience to the will of God, and conceiving God incarnate, are not really commensurable activities. Moreover, all human co-operation with the will of God is possible only because of the grace which God has already given us; and in Mary's case, the grace to do God's will follows precisely from the grace which enables her to be the Godbearer and the grace which follows from that task and office. So the physical act of Godbearing takes priority over everything else that a theologian might want to consider in Mary's life, including her moral virtues.

It is Mary's action as Godbearer, then, which dominates Suárez's entire understanding of her theological importance. We have alrady seen that he puts forward an unusual view concerning Mary's physical motherhood, namely, the view which holds that the flesh that Christ received from his mother, and which, when he was born, made up his entire body – this flesh, which Christ received from his mother at birth, was never lost or destroyed, but always remained as a constituent part of the adult body of Jesus of Nazareth. According to the biological theory that Suárez uses, in the normal process of maturation, the flesh that a child receives from its mother is gradually dissolved, and is replaced by new flesh; and the amount of new flesh also increases to enlarge the overall size of the body. But in the case of Christ, Suárez thinks, this process did not occur in quite the same way: the flesh that Christ received from Mary was not dissolved, but remained always present as a part of his body. This is how it is that, at the Resurrection, the flesh of Mary is a part of the risen body of Christ.[24] And Mary's body, assumed into heaven, is likewise the same flesh as that which is still present in her Son.[25]

In this shared flesh of Christ and his mother, there is a solidarity or continuity that is reminiscent of the union that exists between the Persons of the Trinity. Ramon Llull explains that, when the world is contemplated aright, it is seen that the true being of any one thing resides in the other, and the true being of the other resides in the first. In this sense, the world is created in the image of the Trinity, in whom the true being of each person resides in the other.[26] In the created world, this 'true being' is in fact the God who is the source and end of all things. Suárez's image of the flesh of Mary remaining always in Christ seems to be a graphic illustration of this perception. It says, furthermore, that this union not only exists between creatures, but, since Mary's flesh is in solidarity with all other matter, it exists also between God and creation. The being of the one is always present in the other, so that heaven and earth always dwell each in the other.

Discipleship

In the last 30 years, however, it has often been Mary's discipleship, rather than her motherhood, which has been the subject of Catholic mariology, and more especially, of Marian devotional writing. Indeed, there will be some readers who will be surprised that I have not yet broached the subject of Mary as disciple. So I turn now to explain why I consider this topic to be of only secondary importance when compared with the divine motherhood.

The trend towards an increasing focus on Mary's discipleship has been strongly associated with recent biblical scholarship – most notably, that of the late Raymond Brown (1928–98).[27] Those who focus on Mary as a disciple usually argue either that she is the first, or exemplary, disciple; or that her other attributes and blessings, including her motherhood, are a consequence of her discipleship; or both these things. Briefly, the argument for Mary's discipleship is as follows.

In Luke's Gospel, there are a number of indicators of what it is that Christ requires of his disciples: there are certain qualities which characterize, or are expected of, a disciple of Jesus. At the same time, Luke portrays Mary as possessing precisely these qualities – and possessing them to an excellent degree. The texts that are most commonly cited as exemplifying Mary's discipleship are Luke 8.19–21 and Luke 11.27–28, both taken in conjunction with the Annunciation narrative, Luke 1.26–38.

Luke 8 recounts that Jesus' mother and brothers came to find him while he was preaching to a crowd of people. But because of the crowd they could not reach him:

And he was told, 'Your mother and brothers are standing outside, desiring to see you.' But he said to them, 'My mother and brothers are those who hear the word of God and do it.'

The apparent contrast here between Jesus' natural mother and brothers and those who hear the word of God and do it is ironic. For when Mary said to the angel Gabriel, 'Let it be to me according to your word,' she was precisely hearing the word of God and doing it – and this was the very action by which she became Jesus' mother. So Mary's acceptance of God's word and her consequent motherhood of Christ constitute the archetype or paradigm of those whom Jesus identifies as being close to him. This is then taken by recent Catholic commentators to be the model of Christian discipleship.

In Luke 11.27–28, Jesus is again speaking to a crowd; and on this occasion, a woman cries out, 'Blessed is the womb that bore you, and the breasts that you sucked!' But Jesus responds: 'Blessed rather are those who hear the word of God and keep it!' Once again, it is argued, there is an irony in the apparent contrast between, on the one hand, the physical mother, and on the other, those who keep God's word. For it is precisely because Mary heard the word of God and kept it that her womb bore Christ and her breasts nursed him. So, it seems, Jesus asserts that the moral action of keeping God's word is more important to our beatitude than is our physical condition or our blood relationships; and at the same time we see that it is Mary's moral action of assenting to God's will that enabled her to become Jesus' mother. On this basis, it is argued that Mary's discipleship precedes her motherhood. But there are many difficulties with this line of argument, and I now draw attention to what seem to be one or two of its weaknesses.

In the gospels, Mary is never explicitly referred to as a disciple, but she is clearly designated as Jesus' mother. And whilst a disciple is one who *follows* – who *comes after* – a mother is one who *precedes* – who *comes before*. Now it is true that Mary comes both before and after; in Acts 1 she is present after the Ascension with the church in Jerusalem. But when she gives her assent to Gabriel's message in Luke 1 – the instance usually cited as the paradigmatic case of discipleship – Jesus of Nazareth has not yet even been conceived, let alone begun to assemble disciples around him. On the contrary, it is Mary's action in doing God's will and conceiving Christ that makes all Christian discipleship possible. It is her motherhood that is at the foundation of discipleship, and not the other way round. This is not to deny that Mary may also be a disciple: it is merely to say that her motherhood comes first. It is true that Mary hears the word of God and does it. It is also true that Christian disciples are called to do the same thing. But it does not follow that Mary is thereby a disciple.

Furthermore, if we look more closely at Luke 11.27–28 – where the woman cries out in the crowd, 'Blessed is the womb that bore you and the breasts that you sucked,' – we shall see that Jesus' response is not a general statement about the relative moral worth of discipleship as compared with motherhood: rather, it is an urgent directive which takes for granted the desirability of motherhood and the power of a mother's love for her child. I shall argue this point by reading the passage in question in conjunction with another in Luke's Gospel: Luke 23.27–30. I make this comparison because the two passages have several striking features in common.

Luke 23 is from the account of the Passion, when Jesus is being led to the cross:

> And there followed him a great multitude of the people, and of women who bewailed and lamented him. But Jesus turning to them said, 'Daughters of Jerusalem, do not weep for me, but weep for yourselves and for your children. For behold, the days are coming when they will say, "Blessed are the barren, and the wombs that never bore, and the breasts that never gave suck!" Then they will begin to say to the mountains, "Fall on us"; and to the hills, "Cover us."'

Both these passages – that from Luke 11 and that from Luke 23 – refer to wombs giving birth and to nursing breasts; and both of them use the word μακάριος [makarios], 'blessed', in a negative relationship to those things. That is the first thing they have in common: indeed, 23.29 seems to refer directly back to 11.27. Second, in the two cases, Jesus' injunction follows a similar pattern: in Chapter 11, the woman praises him by reference to his mother, and Jesus responds by turning her attention away from himself and his mother, and telling the woman what she herself should do – namely, hear the word of God and keep it. On the way to Calvary, again, when the women weep for him, Jesus turns their attention away from himself and asks them to concentrate instead on their own condition. So that is a second point the two passages have in common. And finally, the Lord's injunction in both these cases is followed by his giving a prophecy about future destruction or punishment – perhaps about the end of the world. When the woman in the crowd cries out, 'Blessed is the womb that bore you,' the incident is followed by Jesus saying, 'This generation is an evil generation,' and foretelling that it will be judged by the men of Nineveh and the Queen of the South. The teaching about imminent catastrophe is taken up again by Christ on the way to Calvary: 'The days are coming when ... they will say to the mountains, "Fall on us,"' and so on. Taking these two passages together, then, I suggest that we should interpret them as follows.

Jesus foresees a time coming shortly when the world is sunk in violence and cruelty and when it will come under judgement. He takes it for granted that to bear children is normally experienced as a blessing, and that a mother's attachment to her offspring is amongst the strongest on earth. And it is these assumptions which give force to Jesus' assertion that things are going to become so bad that when a mother sees the suffering of her children, or when other people see the horrors around them, they will say, 'It would have been better to be barren than to endure this.' Christ apparently takes it for granted that childbearing is considered to be a great blessing, since the fact that barrenness will be regarded as preferable to motherhood is a measure of how appalling will be the terrible days that are to come. What horrors will a mother see her children become involved in?

Well, Jesus himself is brought to a wretched and horrific death. So when the woman in the crowd cries out how fortunate his mother is, he knows that the time is coming when his mother will be among the most unfortunate women on earth. In times such as these – times of atrocity – an activity and a condition which should be one of the greatest blessings that God has given us – that of motherhood – becomes accursed. How, then, are we to live under such circumstances? What can save us from such horror? According to Christ, all we can do is strive to hear the word of God and keep it: for there is no salvation apart from God's own self, which is his word.

And the words that the Lord gives us in Luke's Gospel must be at least as true today as they were 2000 ago. How blessed was it to be a mother in Rwanda or Kosovo in the 1990s, or in Palestine today? But of course, we do not have to look so far afield to find instances of extreme violence. A chaplain to a high-security prison told of an incident that had occurred there: one of the inmates had committed a particularly horrific murder; and the murderer's mother went to visit her son in prison and said to him, 'It would be better if you were dead.'[28] And what of the victim's mother? Did she in her misery feel that it would be better if she had not borne children?

These are things that could happen to any of us. So let us not suppose that the Lord is moralizing about the worthiness of discipleship and lightly dismissing the importance of motherhood, of kinship, or of human affection. On the contrary, he knows their importance all too well. And he also knows humanity's vulnerability: our capacity for pain, our mortality, and the tenderness of our emotions; and it is for that reason – to show what finally is the only thing possible in a world of terror – that he appeals to his hearers to attend first to the word of God – as, indeed, his own mother did.

It follows from this that if devotion that seems to be given to Our Lord or Our Lady – or any other devotion – takes people away from the fundamental concern for their relationship with God, then there is something wrong with that devotion. Conversely, since God is the beginning from whom we come and the end for whom we are made, anything that helps us on our way towards closer union with God must be right. Christian discipleship is a path towards that end. But we must not think that discipleship is that end in itself. For God calls humanity not just to *follow* Christ, but to enter into union with him and with the Blessed Trinity. Mary may show us much about discipleship: but most of all, she shows us what is its goal. For she has been joined to God more perfectly than any other created human person in the history of the world, and so she shows us the glory that humanity is capable of.

Moreover, it should be borne in mind that not everyone can be a disciple. Most understandings of discipleship imply that it involves an act of *will* – that it is freely chosen, and undertaken as a moral responsibility – which means that it cannot be undertaken by someone who does not have the use of free will, such as a small baby or someone with a severe learning difficulty. Discipleship, therefore, cannot be universal. Fortunately, however, mental capabilities do not determine a person's capacity for union with God. With regard to those of us who are able to be disciples, discipleship is the primary mode in which we approach that greater goal. Yet I suggest that to those who are incapable of discipleship, God nonetheless gives the possibility of attaining the same beatitude that the disciple strives for – a beatitude that is most perfectly accomplished in Mary, in her unique union with the Deity.

St Paul speaks of Christians 'putting on' Christ (Galatians 3.27). But this is possible only because Christ first 'put on' Mary, and thus became a worker in the gold of all human flesh. Paul also writes of Christ filling the whole creation and becoming all in all (Ephesians 1.22–23), and it is Mary who supremely manifests the glory that the rest of the material world, whether or not is not capable of moral choice, awaits as its final destiny.

Nuptial union

So far, then, I have written about the Virgin's union with God by reference to her motherhood. But in recent centuries it has become increasingly popular to think about Mary's relationship with God in terms of spousal imagery, so that the union that takes place between God and Mary is seen as a nuptial one. As with Mary's discipleship, this motif is really of secondary importance. Bridal imagery has been applied to Mary in relation to Christ from the time of the early Christian writers (see below, p. 119), and since she conceives Christ by the Holy Spirit, she has sometimes been referred to in poetry or devotion as 'bride' or 'spouse' of the Holy Spirit. In the modern period, mariologists have sometimes presented Mary also as the spouse of God the Father, because she is the mother of God the Son.[29] Following the work of the nineteenth-century German theologian Matthias Scheeben (1835–88),[30] the bridal motif has had a certain vogue in Marian theology down to the present day, and crops up, for example, in the writings of Hans Urs von Balthasar.[31] Yet Suárez's maternal mariology, outlined above, is superior not only to a mariology based principally on discipleship, but also to one based principally upon the image of nuptial union. Certainly, there are homiletic or narrowly devotional contexts in which it is appropriate to use such imagery – for example, when texts from the Song of Songs have been applied to the Blessed Virgin in a symbolic manner.[32] As to whether or not it is appropriate to speak of the Christian soul's relationship with God in terms of nuptial imagery – more particularly, whether the motif of sexual union can be helpfully applied to that ultimate union with God which is the goal of Christian life – here also, there may be occasions on which such imagery can be properly employed, but we need to exercise a great deal of caution in our use of it.

God cannot adequately be spoken of in the language of objects or categories within the created order, and it is always incumbent upon us to speak of God in ways which respect that inadequacy. The danger of trying to understand a creature's union with God as analogous to sexual union is that we might suppose God to have the attributes of created gender – usually, of masculinity.

The mariologist René Laurentin has spoken of the limitations of referring to Mary as spouse of the Holy Spirit, since this language suggests that we are dealing with a pagan myth in which male gods have sexual intercourse with human women. Laurentin says:

According to the whole of Tradition, [the Holy Spirit's] role with respect to Mary is not a face to face one. With her, as with us, he awakens each from the inside, from their best self: in Mary's case to the supreme accomplishment of her ... maternal capabilities, to become

Mother of God ... . He is the transcendental principle of a conception that is completely virginal without any external contribution, in the image of generation by the Father. This is important if we are not to misconceive the transcendent roles of the Father and the Spirit, as well as the temporal role of Mary.[33]

To understand Mary's, or anyone else's, relationship with God by means of the imagery of nuptial union is thus highly problematical. Mary's union with God in the divine motherhood, on the other hand, is much less so. This is because the divine motherhood is not a comprehensible metaphor for an incomprehensible reality: it is from the outset an incomprehensible mystery in itself. This means that we are not presented with the danger of reifying, or making concrete, a symbolic motif; and the paradox of the Incarnation, signified in the virginal motherhood, constantly warns us off trying to grasp this truth adequately at a human level. The union with God, which is the creature's proper destiny, must likewise be understood to incorporate a transcendent element that we cannot now comprehend.

Apart from the foregoing considerations, the union of bodies which occurs in sexual intercourse is not as complete as the union of flesh which exists between a pregnant woman and the child gestating in her womb, and is thus not such a good representation of that union with God which undergirds the universe, which all men and women are called to realize, and whose realization is made possible by Mary's motherhood. Christianity's principal guarantee of God's creative and redemptive presence throughout the cosmos is given in the doctrine that he was conceived and grew in the womb of his mother Mary, and was born of her. It is this relationship which shows the world's true likeness to the Blessed Trinity, and its capacity to reveal that likeness most fully. For Christ is always a worker in the gold of creation's flesh.

Notes

1 Taken from Palmeira, R. (ed.), *In the Gold of Flesh: Poems of Birth and Motherhood*, The Women's Press, London, 1990, 21.
2 Steingraber, S., *Having Faith*, The Perseus Press, Oxford, 2002, 33–6.
3 Contained in a work popularly known as *De Mysteriis Vitae Christi*, which is part of Suárez's commentary on the *Summa Theologica* of Thomas Aquinas: *Commentarii et disputationes in tertiam partem D. Thomae, quaestiones 27–59*, in *Opera Omnia*, ed. Berton, C., Vol. 19,

Disputations I-XXIII, Vivès, Paris, 1860, 1–337. An English transla-
tion of Disputations I, V and VI can be found in Suárez, F., *The
Dignity and Virginity of the Mother of God*, (trans. R. O'Brien), West
Baden College, West Baden Springs, Indiana, 1954.

4 Suárez, F., *Comm.*, Vol. XIX, disp.I, 3.

5 Suárez, F., *Comm.*, Vol. XIX, disp.I, sec.I:9, 5.

6 Suárez, F., *Comm.*, Vol. XIX, disp.I, sec.II:2, 7.

7 *Ibid.*

8 *Ibid.*

9 The most substantial biography of Suárez is de Scoraille, R., *François
Suárez de la Compagnie de Jésus, d'après ses lettres, ses autres écrits
inédits et un grand nombre de documents nouveaux*, 2 vols,
Lethielleux, Paris, 1912.

10 The importance of Suárez's thought for the whole development of
Western metaphysics has been brilliantly argued by Jean-François
Courtine: *Suárez et le Système de la Métaphysique*, Presses
Universitaires de France, Paris, 1990.

11 Suárez, F., *De Legibus*, Vol. I: *De natura legis* (ed. Luciano Pereña, *et
al.*; Latin text with Spanish translation), Consejo Superior de
Investigaciones Cientificas, Madrid, 1971 (Vol. XI of Corpus
Hispanorum de Pace), 2–3.

12 Suárez, F., *Comm.*, Vol XIX, disp.I, sec.II:7, 9–10.

13 Wolter, A. B., and O'Neill, B., *John Duns Scotus: Mary's Architect*,
Franciscan Press, Quincy, Illinois, 1993, 49–54. Wolter and O'Neill
consider that 'Scotus was not primarily concerned with what God
might have done … if Adam had not sinned'; rather, 'he began with
… the fact of the Incarnation as it actually occurred in all its details.
And thus Scotus also takes into account that the complete motive for
Christ's Incarnation includes also the prevision of Adam's fall and his
subsequent redemption' (p.49). The more usual reading of Scotus
highlights his teaching that the Incarnation was predestined from
before the prevision of Adam's fall, and this is the teaching that
appears in Suárez's teaching on the Blessed Virgin's predestination
to be Mother of God.

14 Suárez, F., *Comm.*, Vol XIX, disp.I, sec.III:4, 11.

15 Suárez, F., *Comm.*, Vol XIX, disp.I, sec.III:1–4, 10–11.

16 Suárez, F., *Comm.*, Vol XIX, disp.IV, sec. I:3–4, 56–7.

17 See Boss, S.J., *Empress and Handmaid: On Nature and Gender in
the Cult of the Virgin Mary*, Cassell, London, 2000, 34–6.

18 Southwell, R., 'The Conception of Our Ladie', in Jennings, E. (ed.), *In Praise of Our Lady*, Batsford, London, 1982, 19.

19 I am grateful to John Montag SJ, for pointing out to me that Suárez's assertion of the continued union of Christ's and Mary's flesh is probably a point about substance.

20 Suárez, F., *Comm.*, Vol. XIX, Praefatio, 1, 1.

21 In Renaissance painting, the St Anne Trinity is sometimes depicted as St Anne and the Virgin seated with Christ between them, and directly above him are shown God the Father and the Holy Spirit. Christ thus simultaneously forms part of a vertical and of a horizontal triad, indicating both his human and divine origins. The visual correspondence between the two 'Trinities' gives a strong sense of there being a parallel between the divine and the earthly. See Pamela Sheingorn: 'Appropriating the Holy Kinship: Gender and family history', in Ashley, K. and Sheingorn, P. (eds.), *Interpreting Cultural Symbols: St. Anne in Late Medieval Society*, The University of Georgia Press, Athens and London, 1990, 169–98, at 176–8.

22 Nasr, S. H., *Religion and the Order of Nature*, Oxford University Press, New York, 1996.

23 Bernard of Clairvaux, [Homily on the Annunciation] Homily I:5–6, in Bernard of Clairvaux and Amadeus of Lausanne, *Magnificat: Homilies in Praise of the Blessed Virgin Mary* (trans. M.-B. Saïd and G. Perigo,) Cistercian Publications, Kalamazoo, Michigan, 1979, 9–10.

24 Suárez, F., *Comm.*, Vol XIX, disp.I, sec.II:2, 7–8.

25 Suárez, F., *Comm.*, Vol XIX, disp.XXI, sec.II:6, 317.

26 Vega, A., *Rámon Llull y el Secreto de la Vida*, Ediciones de Siruela, Madrid, 2000, 62.

27 See especially Brown, R.E. *et al.*, *Mary in the New Testament*, Geoffrey Chapman, London, 1978, and Brown, R.E., *The Birth of the Messiah: A Commentary on the Infancy Narratives in the Gospels of Matthew and Luke*, Geoffrey Chapman, London, 1993. The arguments of these works sum up earlier scholarship on the subject.

28 Incident narrated to the author in conversation.

29 For example, Olier, J.-J., *Vie Intérieure de la Très Sainte Vierge* [collected from Olier's writings], Vol. 1, Salviucci, Rome, 1866, 53–66.

30 Scheeben, M., *Mariology*, Vol. 1 (trans. T.L.M.J. Geukers), Herder Book Co., St Louis and London, 1946, 154–83.

31 A description of this and other motifs in von Balthasar's writing on Mary is given in Leahy, B., *The Marian Profile in the Ecclesiology of*

Hans Urs von Balthasar, New City, London, 2000.

32 For a helpful survey of these applications, see Warner, M., *Alone of All Her Sex: The Myth and the Cult of the Virgin Mary*, Picador, London, 1990, 121–33.

33 Laurentin, R., 'Mary and the Holy Spirit', in Plunkett, D. (ed.), *The Virgin Mary and the People of God* (proceedings of a symposium, 29–31 May, 1998), Maryvale Institute, Birmingham, 1998, 32–40, at 34–5.

5
The Sacred Vessel

To the modern reader, one of the most engaging parts of the Bible is the story of the life of King David, told in the first and second books of Samuel. David is the second king of Israel. He is the king who unites the tribes of Israel and who conquers Jerusalem, the city on the holy mountain of Zion, making it the political and religious capital of the nation. Jerusalem becomes the dwelling-place of God. Ever since the days of Moses, when the tribes of Israel were wandering in the wilderness, the people have carried with them the ark of the Covenant, the mysterious dwelling-place of the Lord, the unseen God who cannot be contained by vessels of any kind. But David, amidst much rejoicing and merrymaking, brings the ark to Jerusalem, where David's son Solomon will eventually build a splendid temple to house it. On the way, however, as David and his men carry the ark on an ox-cart to the holy city, a terrifying incident occurs. One of the oxen transporting the sacred vessel stumbles in the road, and one of the men present, by the name of Uzzah, puts out his hand and takes hold of the ark. But, the narrator tells us, 'the anger of the Lord was kindled against Uzzah; and God smote him there because he put forth his hand to the ark; and he died there beside the ark of God' (2 Samuel 6.7).

David is completely taken aback by this event, and angry that the Lord has treated Uzzah in this way. He asks, 'How can the ark of the Lord come to me?' (v.9). And David takes the ark aside to the house of a man named Obededom, where it remains for three months, before continuing on its journey to Jerusalem.

This is a story that raises awkward theological questions – as its principal character, King David, recognizes. Why should God strike down a man who was trying to defend his sacred ark? A part of the answer to this is that the ark is an object of exceptional sanctity, and a sacred object has the power to impart both blessing and harm. But let us consider how this passage is alluded to in a later text.

In Luke's gospel, the account of the Visitation, that is, the pregnant Mary's visit to her cousin Elizabeth (Luke 1.39–56), seems to be strongly

influenced by the narrative of 2 Samuel 6. Immediately after the
Annunciation and the conception of Jesus, Mary goes to visit Elizabeth,
who is also expecting a child, the future John the Baptist. When the two
women greet one another, Elizabeth proclaims Mary 'blessed among
women', and says, 'And why is this granted me, that the mother of my
Lord should come to me?' (v.43). Mary sings her great song of rejoicing,
popularly known by its first word in Latin, the *Magnificat*, and at the end
of the narrative, we are told that 'Mary remained with Elizabeth about
three months'. Elizabeth's question as to why the mother of her Lord
should come to her seems to echo David's question as to how the ark of the
Lord could come to him; and the time of Mary's stay at her cousin's is the
same as the time that the ark remains in the house of Obededom. It seems
as if Luke wants the reader to understand that Mary bears within her the
presence of the Lord, as does the ark of God. She is the vessel in whom the
uncontainable God mysteriously dwells. She too is infused with the most
powerful holiness.

To readers in the twenty-first century, the image of a vessel may seem
to be of little moral significance. The viciousness of our attitude towards
other creatures is such that containers – bottles, cartons, plastic bags – are
often made to be thrown away. When their content has been used up, their
value has gone with it. But this has not always been the case. Until
recently, people took their own jugs to collect milk from churns, and
returned glass bottles to the shop to be used again. Vessels were kept and
re-used, not cast aside as 'rubbish'. And far beyond any practical, mone-
tary or sentimental value that everyday containers might have, the Old
Testament narratives concerning the ark of the Covenant show it to be a
vessel of the most extreme sanctity. It is the bearer of God.

In Catholic tradition, the sacred vessel is a primary category of experience and sensibility.[1] In the early Church, the Eucharist – the symbolic
meal that was the principal act of Christian worship – was celebrated over
the tombs of martyrs, that is, on a container bearing the body of holy men
or women. In continuation of this practice, altars still contain the relics of
saints, and an altar is thus a sacred vessel. For this reason, altars were,
until recently, made in the shape of tombs. Every Catholic church has
within it a tabernacle, the box which contains a host – bread that has been
consecrated at Mass as the body of Christ. Many churches contain reliquaries bearing the remains of saints, and the reliquaries are often lavishly
decorated with precious metals and stones as a sign of the high status of their
contents. Most central, perhaps, are the sacred vessels used for celebrating the

eucharist – the chalice for the blood of Christ, and the paten for Christ's body. These are supposed to be made of precious metals and, as has been mentioned above, are kept and cleaned separately from profane objects. The most sacred vessel of all would be the Holy Grail, the original chalice of Christ's blood, which is proverbial for that which is most sought after. In Chapter Two we saw that, in the legend of the quest for the Grail, the vessel takes on something of the identity of its sacred occupant, and this is a characteristic of all sacred vessels. The container is holy because it has once borne holy contents.

Now, if all the vessels named above are holy, then the most sacred of all vessels must be the Virgin Mary. She bore God incarnate in her own body; and more than this, she gave her own flesh to be his flesh. In addition, she freely co-operated in this work and was active in bringing about the miracle.

We have already seen that Luke compares Mary to the ark of the Lord. But in Luke's thought, there are more connotations than this to Mary's office as vessel of the divine. It is good to read Luke together with the book of the Acts of the Apostles, since they are written by the same author and display similar concerns. The book of Acts contains the story of the giving of the Holy Spirit at Pentecost, and it is reasonable to think of Luke's Gospel as being written in the light of this event. The author has recorded the memories of Jesus held by the first Christian community in Jerusalem (the community mentioned at the beginning of Acts), interpreted in the light of the experience not only of Christ's resurrection and ascension, but also of God's extraordinary gift of the Holy Spirit, since these are the events that reveal the meaning of all that has gone before.

The book of Acts begins with the story of Christ's ascension into heaven, forty days after his resurrection from the dead. After this, Jesus' disciples, including his brothers and his mother Mary, are in the habit of meeting together for prayer (Acts 1.14). Then, on the day of the feast of Pentecost, the little band of Christians is gathered together in this way when they experience something like a rushing wind in the room. After this, tongues of fire appear, and rest on the heads of each person present. The disciples then go out into the streets, where there are people from all around the Eastern Mediterranean, speaking many different languages. The disciples find that when they speak to these people, each of them hears what is said in his or her own language. Everyone, we are told, is amazed. Everyone, that is, except for a few scoffers who say, 'They are drunk on new wine' (Acts 2.1–13). Peter immediately disputes this calumny, pointing out that it is still very early in the morning. Yet those who make the accusation may well be uttering a true word spoken in jest. For if we look back to Luke's Gospel, we find a parable told by Jesus, which, in its immediate context, makes little sense, but which might well be interpreted in the light of the gift of tongues:

> No one puts new wine into old wineskins; if he does, the new wine will burst the skins and it will be spilled, and the skins will be destroyed. But new wine must be put into fresh wineskins. (Luke 5.37–38)

Surely the 'new wine' is the gift of the Holy Spirit? It is the new life that is bestowed upon Christians and which brings the Church into being at Pentecost. The disciples in Jerusalem are, in a certain sense, filled with new wine – but it is the new wine of the Spirit, not the grape, and the Christians' apparent intoxication is of spiritual origin.

Note that, according to the parable, new wine can be put only into wineskins that are *fresh*. This points us to one aspect of the meaning of Mary's virginity in the narrative of the Annunciation (Luke 1.26–38). We have seen that this motif takes us back to the dawn of creation, when the Spirit of God broods over the face of the formless deep, and the world awaits God's creative word. In Luke's account, Mary is overshadowed by the Holy Spirit and conceives the Son of God in her body. She thus receives the new wine of salvation in a unique manner: more perfectly and more intimately than anyone else in the story of salvation. It is only that which is completely new that can receive the new wine of the Spirit, and Mary in her virginity is the founding of the new vessel. Mary is the fresh wineskin *par excellence*: she receives the Holy Spirit, and nurtures and gives forth Christ himself. What happens to the Church at Pentecost is a continuation of what happens to Mary at the Annunciation. Overshadowed by the Holy Spirit, it is a vessel filled with the new life of Christ.

The idea that Mary is the one who first becomes the dwelling-place of God so that we too might become habitations of God's presence is an idea that has been given very beautiful expression in Christian tradition. Saint Francis of Assisi (1181–1226), for example, wrote this prayer, 'A Salutation of the Blessed Virgin Mary':

> Hail, O Lady,
> Holy Queen,
> Mary, holy Mother of God,
> who are the Virgin made Church,

chosen by the most Holy Father in Heaven
whom he consecrated with His most holy beloved Son
and with the Holy Spirit the Paraclete,
in whom there was and is
all fullness of grace and every good.

Hail His Palace!
Hail His Tabernacle!
Hail His Dwelling!
Hail His Robe!
Hail His Servant!
Hail His Mother!

And hail all you holy virtues
which are poured into the hearts of the faithful
through the grace and enlightenment of the Holy Spirit,
that from being unbelievers,
You may make them faithful to God.[2]

It is in devotion attached to the Eucharist, however, that the image of Mary as sacred vessel appears most strongly. In the teaching of the Catholic and Orthodox churches, Christ is again really present in the bread and wine that is consecrated by the priest to be eaten and drunk as communion during the ceremony that is called 'Mass' by Catholics, and the 'Liturgy' by the Orthodox. In scriptural accounts of Christ's last supper with his apostles, he says, 'Take, eat, this is my body,' and 'Take, drink, this is my blood'. These words are the words of consecration spoken by the priest in the liturgy itself, which is, amongst other things, a memorial of that meal. The doctrine of the 'real presence' means that both the humanity and divinity of Christ are made present again to the faithful during the eucharistic celebration. For many hundreds of years, it was common for there to be a painting or statue of the Virgin and Child above the main altar of a church, and this served as a reminder that the body and blood which had once been given to Christ by his mother Mary were again made present on the altar during Mass.

In fact, the structure of the liturgy has a certain correspondence with that of Christ's incarnation. During the eucharistic prayer, before the words of consecration, the priest calls down the Holy Spirit with the words, 'Let your Spirit come upon these gifts to make them holy.' And in a certain sense, the coming down of the Holy Spirit upon the elements of the eucharist (the bread and the wine) is the same thing as the overshadowing of the Virgin at the Annunciation. At the Annunciation, the Spirit comes upon Mary, and Christ is conceived by the word of God through the angel. At Mass, the priest calls down the Holy Spirit, and the real presence of Christ is brought about in the words and other actions that Christ himself used in establishing his commemorative meal. In both places, the Holy Spirit descends, and Christ becomes present in created form.

Mary is the sacred shrine in whom Christ dwells, and the chalice and paten of the eucharist participate in this primary action of Mary. It is because she was once uniquely the sacred vessel who bore Christ that the chalice and paten can now become sacred vessels which also bear Christ. The care with which these vessels are supposed to be looked after is perhaps a constant returning of them to the state of 'new wineskins', or a virginal condition, in which they will again be able to receive the living Lord.

Mary's association with the eucharistic vessels is expressed very eloquently in a thirteenth-century text from Worcester Cathedral. It is an antiphon that was written to be sung during the reception of communion. In translation, it says:

Blessed womb
 of the Virgin Mary,
Which, heavy with fruit
 seeded in eternity,
Diligently carried
 for us, humanity,
In the cup of life
 the drink of all sweetness.

As Mary carried the living God in her body, so the living God is present for the faithful again in the Eucharist.

St Francis' 'Salutation of the Blessed Virgin Mary' moves from honouring Mary as a vessel who bears God, to praying for holy virtues to be poured into Christian hearts. We too are called to be filled with the Holy Spirit and to be bearers of God in our own lives. To perceive a sound, I must use the faculty of hearing, and to perceive a sight, I must use the faculty of vision. In the same way, if I am to perceive the Godbearing nature of the world around me, I must use a spiritual faculty – the acknowledgment and nurturing of God's presence within myself. The recognition of

God's presence in oneself, and the recognition of God's presence in other creatures, are entailed in one another. And Mary is the archetype of both the Godbearing cosmos and the Godbearing soul.

Notes

1 Hirn, Y., *The Sacred Shrine: A Study of the Poetry and Art of the Catholic Church*, Faber and Faber, London, 1958.
2 Conroy, L., 'The Virgin Mary in the writings of Francis and Clare', *Maria: A Journal of Marian studies* 3(1) (August 2002), 17–70, at 48.

6

The Darkness before the Dawn

Our Lady of Le Puy

The shrine of Our Lady of Le Puy, in the province of Velay in southern France, is home to one of the most famous of the numerous black Madonnas that are found in Europe.[1] It is located in a striking natural setting, where peaks of rock emerge out of what were once thick woodlands. Romantic legend maintains that in ancient times there was a sanctuary on each of the rocky peaks, the most important of which was Mount Anis. On its summit was a dolmen, a single megalith, on which sacrifices were offered to 'the Virgin who would bear a son'. The legend of how this place came to be a shrine of the Virgin Mary runs as follows.

A widow with rheumatic fever went to lie on the stone that was there. During the night, the Virgin appeared to the woman in a vision, and said that she wished for a Christian sanctuary to be built on Mount Anis. When the woman awoke from her sleep, she was cured of the rheumatic fever. So the widow went to see the bishop, George, the man who had first brought the Christian gospel to this region of Gaul, and told him what had happened. Together, the bishop and the widow went back to the mountain, and, although it was a hot day in July, the summit was covered with snow. As they stood there, a stag leapt out of a thicket and ran around the rock on which the stone lay, leaving hoof marks in the snow. Although the miraculous events confirmed the truth of the widow's vision, Bishop George could not afford to build a church; but he planted a hawthorn hedge in the stag's footprints, to mark out the sacred territory. The next morning, the snow was gone, but the hawthorn was in bloom, making a 'snowy crown' on the mountain top. Clearly, this place was sacred to the Virgin Mary. It was consecrated by another bishop, St Martial, who brought there a relic of the Virgin, one of her shoes.

Gradually, the hawthorn hedge grew into a grove, and pilgrims would come to spend the night there, sleeping on the sacred stone. Amongst these, in the year 350, was a paralytic woman, to whom the Virgin also appeared in a vision, and who was also healed of her infirmity. She too went to report her experience to the bishop, whose name was Vosy. By this time, the Church had become wealthier, and Vosy was a rich man who was able to build the first Christian church on this site. One tradition maintains that the bishop and his chaplain happened to meet an old man who supplied them with the relics that they would need to place in the church's altar, and that the next day, when no man or woman was present in the building, the church bells rang, its doors were opened and its windows ablaze with light, because its consecration was being undertaken by angels.

For many centuries, the stone stood in front of the church's high altar (presumably because the altar was built by the site where the stone already lay). Steps led directly up to it from outside the building. Nowadays, however, there is an ordinary floor in the nave, and the stone has been placed by the door. The custom of spending the night on the stone was still carried out at least as recently as a hundred years ago. Frances Gostling, an English traveller in France in 1911, wrote of Le Puy:

And when you have knelt and made your prayer on the stone, you ascend to the Lady of the Stone, the Mother of Health and Healing. A beautiful symbol, is it not, the Druid altar a Marche Pied leading to the Virgin herself? The old religion conducting to the new?[2]

This is a legend rich in natural symbolism: the sacred mountain in its woodland, the healing stone, the hawthorn grove and the stag are all signs of the divine presence in this chosen place. The idea that this was a prophetically sacred spot even before the advent of Christianity, or a 'Druid' shrine, is also significant, not so much for its historical claim (which is almost certainly awry) as for the importance that it holds as a myth for us today.

But at Le Puy, it is not only the site that is enveloped in sacred mythology, but also the statue of the Virgin and Child. According to tradition, this too is a pre-Christian image prophetic of Christianity. The original statue is said to have been carved by the Hebrew prophet Jeremiah, while he remained in Egypt after fleeing there following the fall of Jerusalem. The statue is thus a visual prophecy of the Incarnation. One tradition recounts that King St Louis IX of France, on his way to Palestine to join a Crusade, was captured by the Sultan of Egypt. Whilst he was there awaiting his ransom, the sultan showed him many of the treasures of his country, amongst which, in the Temple, was a black statue of a mother and child.

King Louis immediately recognized the image as a statue of the Virgin and Christ. When the king's ransom arrived, the sultan told him that he could choose a gift, from everything he had seen in Egypt, to take back with him to his native land, and the gift that Louis chose was the statue of the mother and child. The sultan was most reluctant to let it go, but, having given his word, he could not go back on it, and so the statue was taken by Louis to France, where it was given to the shrine of Le Puy.

An older version of this story,[3] however, recounts that Jeremiah made the statue in Jerusalem, before the destruction of the Temple by Nebuchadnezzar, and that at the fall of Jerusalem it was taken to the treasury in Babylon. It was eventually brought to France by a Catholic king returning from pilgrimage to the Holy Land, long before the time of the Crusades. The French king received hospitality from the Sultan of Babylon who asked him to choose a gift before he left, and the king chose the statue of the Virgin and Child. On his outward journey to the East, he had passed through Le Puy, and on his return, he presented the statue to the shrine there.

After the French Revolution, with the desecration of many holy places, the statue of Our Lady of Le Puy was burnt in 1794. The present statue is a copy of the original. Fortunately, at the time of the statue's destruction, a detailed description and drawing of it was made by an antiquarian, Faujas de Saint-Fond. The account by Faujas de Saint-Fond suggests to art historians that the image was a Virgin in Majesty, similar to that of Our Lady of Orcival (frontispiece), probably dating from the twelfth century.[4] Faujas de Saint-Fond, however, believed it to be a statue of the Egyptian goddess Isis with her son Horus, brought to France from Egypt in the mistaken belief that it represented Christ and the Virgin.

A Book of Hours (daily prayer used by lay people) from the end of the fifteenth century contains an illumination depicting the Virgin of Le Puy. She is represented as black, and this illustration may be the earliest surviving representation of a black Virgin.[5]

Black Virgins: their character and origins

So what is the definition of a black Virgin? Where are they found? And why are they black?

The first use of the term 'black Virgin' seems to have been in France during the nineteenth century. It referred to those statues of the Virgin Mary that were painted black, even though the local populations – who were predominantly French – were white. And indeed, *an image of the Virgin Mary coloured black or dark brown, in a place where the local population is white*, makes quite a good initial definition of a black Virgin. It is true that there are some 'black Virgins' in places where the native population is dark-skinned, but these usually have some connection to Europe. For example, the famous image of Our Lady of Guadalupe in Mexico City, who has the features of the local Indian population, is named after the black Virgin of Guadalupe in Extremadura, Spain.

Our definition has to be qualified, however, by the puzzling fact that there are a few images commonly called 'black Virgins' that are painted in the flesh tones of the local white inhabitants. Our Lady of Orcival, in the diocese of Clermont in the French province of Auvergne, is one such example (frontispiece). It is as though the word 'black' has some metaphorical meaning that is not bound to the colour of the actual image. The safest definition of a black Virgin is probably *an image of the Virgin Mary whose devotees commonly refer to her as 'black'*.

Black Virgins are found in many places – the icon of Our Lady of Czestochowa in Poland, for example, is usually thought of as 'the Black Madonna', and the statue of Nossa Senhora Aparecida, the patroness of Brazil, is also a black Madonna. France is particularly rich in black Virgin statues, and much of the literature on the subject of black Madonnas maintains that France is the single nation with the largest number, if not an absolute majority, of the world's black Virgins. However, we need to be a little sceptical of this claim. The French have provided most of the scholarship on this subject, and, naturally, French scholars have tended to focus predominantly on the images in their own country. Yet Spain and Italy are certainly not lacking in black Virgins. However, there seem to be no specialist studies of black Madonnas in those countries,[6] let alone any thorough international study of the phenomenon.[7]

The most intriguing question, of course, concerns the reason for the images' blackness. 'Why is she black?' asks the surprised visitor to a European shrine. And the answers are many and varied. The traditional answer from clergy or church officials has tended to be that the image became blackened with candle smoke or other dirt collected over time. Yet even if this account were true in origin, it would not explain why it is that the statue has gone on being painted black, rather than being restored to its original white. This, after all, is what has been done with the statues of other saints – and other Madonnas – when they have become grubby.

One of the most persuasive arguments for the origins of black

Madonnas is that put forward by Sophie Cassagnes-Brouquet,[8] following in the footsteps of the great folklorist Emile Saillens,[9] who points out that the dispersion of black Virgins in France is most dense in the south-east and the centre, whilst there are very few black Virgins in the north and west of the country. This means that black Virgins occur most commonly in the part of France that was most heavily influenced by classical culture. The trade route from the Mediterranean up the Rhône Valley in ancient times ensured that cultural influences from Africa and the East could always find their way into Gaul, and the influx of wider Mediterranean culture became particularly strong during the period of the Greek colony at Marseilles (founded about 600 BC), followed by the Roman occupation which eventually spread to the whole country. In classical antiquity, black was sometimes used as a colour for statues of people of exceptional importance, and there were some goddesses who could be represented as black – most notably, perhaps, Artemis of the Ephesians. According to the argument promoted by Cassagnes-Brouquet, many shrines of black Virgins are on sites previously occupied by the shrines of goddesses.[10] Cassagnes-Brouquet contends, therefore, that the blackness of the Virgin in these places represents a tradition of continuity with the pagan past of the same sites.

Another argument for the origins of the statues' blackness is put forward by Sylvie Vilatte, who holds that statues which were previously white were deliberately painted black in the fourteenth century, as part of a campaign to revive interest in the Crusades. According to this theory, the representation of Christian saints as black was intended to draw the attention of ordinary Europeans to the possibility of converting dark-skinned Moors to Christianity.[11]

Both these theories have some degree of plausibility with regard to the origins of black-coloured Virgin statues, but neither of them says enough to give the whole story. If the statues were painted black in the fourteenth century, then why did people not return them to their original colour at a later time? What was, and is, the attraction of continuing the statues' blackness? Then again, if the Virgins were coloured black in continuity with pagan precedent, the question is similar: why was black considered an appropriate colour for the goddesses, and why did Christians see their blackness as an attribute that they wished, and still wish, to maintain in their images of the Virgin Mary? Do we not have to suppose that there is some spiritual significance to this colour, and that it is in the realm of the spiritual, and not the historical, that the meaning of the black Madonnas must be sought?

Blackness as darkness

In English, 'black' can sometimes be used as a synonym for 'dark'. If I look out of the window on a dark night, I might say, 'It's inky black out there.' Conversely, the words 'dark' and 'dusky' (from *dusk*, meaning twilight) can be used to describe skin colour. In some languages, however, blackness and darkness are quite distinct, and cannot be assimilated to one another in this way: darkness is one thing, and the colour black another. I am going on to suggest that at least some of the significance of black Madonnas depends upon a confusion of these two concepts.

In Western European culture, blackness has often been associated with evil. We speak of 'black magic' or the 'black arts'. The word 'denigrate', meaning to make something appear bad, comes from the Latin *nigrum*, meaning black. Indeed, we can speak straightforwardly of 'blackening' someone's character. At the same time, Europeans have had an ambivalent attitude to dark-skinned people – black, Arab and Asian alike – and have frequently seen them as being in several respects inferior to white-skinned people. In European culture, sacred figures are most commonly of fair complexion (and note the double meaning of the word 'fair', corresponding to the double meaning of its opposite, 'dark', as in the expression, 'Those were dark days'). This may, of course, be due partly to the fact that in a society in which most people have to spend their time toiling in fields, it is only the privileged who can afford to stay indoors and not get weather-beaten brown skin. But this reinforces the point: whiteness or fairness is seen as a desirable condition, whilst blackness or darkness is not.

From this point of view, the representation of the Virgin and Child as black is on the one hand curious, because of the figures' supreme sanctity, yet at the same time may have a Christian rationale. For a constant theme of the Hebrew Scriptures, the Gospels, and Christian teaching through the ages has been God's preference for the poor and the humble, that is to say, for those whom human society despises. In the middle ages it was taught consistently that the rich could enter heaven only by charity towards the poor, and the prayers of the poor were considered highly desirable to help one on the path to salvation. The free choice of poverty for oneself has been presented in the Catholic Church as one of the delineations of the path of spiritual excellence, down to the present day. Likewise, righteous people who suffer physical ailments, and those who adopt an attitude of humility in any aspect of life, are believed to be especially beloved of God. This philosophy is articulated with particular clarity in the song that Mary sings to

her cousin Elizabeth when the two pregnant women meet one another
(Luke 1.46–55). In this song of rejoicing, the *Magnificat*, Mary proclaims
that God has 'cast down the mighty from their seats, and exalted the humble
and meek'. This is what God has done in bringing about the conception of
Christ in Mary's womb. So there is a certain appropriateness about an
image of the Virgin and Child being represented as black, especially since,
in most black Virgin statues, the Virgin is enthroned as a queen. It is as
though the blackness signifies all that human culture mistakenly despises,
and all the people we reject, so that in the black Madonna we see God
raising these things and these people up to a place of honour. In becoming
human, Christ binds himself to every last part of the human condition and
the material world – including the things that we think of as 'black' – and
offers it the possibility of redemption and glorification. In the blackness of
the regal Virgin and Child, the very humblest are exalted.

Many of the black Virgin statues were sculpted during the twelfth and
thirteenth centuries, and a further clue to their spiritual significance may
perhaps be indicated by a contemporary text, the story of *Peredur Son of
Efrawg*, which is included in the Welsh collection *The Maginogion*.[12] The
hero, Peredur, is the Arthurian knight who is the Welsh equivalent of
Percival, and his story has many points in common with Wolfram von
Eschenbach's *Parsifal*, although *Peredur* has the merit of being told in a
more primitive and less ornate style. Peredur's adventures include many
extraordinary experiences. Early on, he is present at the hall of the Lame
King, when two youths proceed through the hall carrying an enormous
spear with three streams of blood running along it. After that, two maid-
ens come through carrying a salver on which there is a man's head surrounded by blood.[13] The reader is given no explanation for this, and
Peredur does not enquire. Indeed, throughout the whole narrative, strange
events occur which seem disconnected from one another. Peredur continues on his way, and carries out many acts of heroism. Eventually, he goes
to seek the hand of the Empress of Constantinople, who desires only the
bravest man, and he succeeds in winning her favour. He rules with her for
fourteen years, before returning to the Court of King Arthur.[14] At several
points in the narrative, Peredur fights with men who are described as
'black'. The final dénouement to the story is at least as strange as everything that has gone before, and one part of it concerns a terrifying woman
called the Black Virgin, *y forwyn ddu*. The Black Virgin challenges
Peredur as to why, when he was at the Court of the Lame King, he did not
question the meaning of the blood-dripping spear. She says that if he

had only asked what this meant, much bloodshed could have been avoided.[15] But he did not, and his failure to ask the right questions has had terrible consequences. So the Black Virgin makes the hero aware of his sins of ommission: she forces him to confront those things in his past which he would prefer to ignore.

Now, the confrontation with past sin is central to the Christian tradition. It is through confession of one's sins and the grace of forgiveness that one breaks one's attachment to the past and is freed to form right relationships with God and one's fellow creatures. The rite of Christian initiation, baptism, is specifically for the forgiveness of sins, and Christ says that we must forgive those who wrong us as many times as they cause us offence. Yet full acknowledgement of past wrong-doing, and even mistakes and other failings, can be painfully difficult, so it is not surprising that the figure who calls the hero to account, the Black Virgin, should be a frightening one.

It may therefore be the case that part of the spiritual meaning of the black Virgin in Christian devotion is likewise one of recalling sin – of becoming aware of that which is 'black' within us, and of confronting 'dark' events in our lives. Certainly, at one of the most important shrines of a black Virgin, Our Lady of Rocamadour, in south-western central France, it was once the custom for pilgrims to travel there specifically as an act of penitence. Ecclesiastical courts in Germany would send malefactors to Rocamadour in chains, and when the prisoners had carried out their rites of expiation at the shrine, their chains would be removed and their freedom restored. King Henry II is said to have expiated the murder of Thomas Becket by doing penance in front of his troops at Rocamadour, and it was once the custom for pilgrims to undertake the penitential gesture of climbing up the steps to the shrine on their knees. So the Virgin's blackness may in part signify her frightening function of summoning us to address our own 'blackness'.

Yet if the Virgin calls us to acknowledge the darkness of sin, this is only in order that, by doing so, we become freed from that sin and are brought out of darkness and into the light of Christ. That is to say, the black Virgin signifies and provokes the process of spiritual enlightenment. This is suggested by a verse of Scripture that is commonly cited in connection with black Madonnas, namely, Song of Songs 1.5. The Song of Songs is a collection of love poetry, traditionally read as a dialogue between the lover, or groom, and the beloved, or bride. In Jewish tradition it has been interpreted as an allegory for the relationship between the Lord and Israel,

whilst Christians have understood it to signify the loving relationship that
exists between Christ and the Church, or Christ and the human soul. Since
Mary is a 'type' of both the Church and the soul in its relationship with
Christ, it became common to attribute to Mary the words of the Song that
are said by and about the Beloved. The Song itself claims to have been
written by King Solomon, and tradition has often understood the original
Lover to be Solomon and the Beloved to be the Queen of Sheba, a wise
monarch who visited King Solomon to discover that his wisdom was even
greater than her own (1 Kings 10.1–13). In Matthew's Gospel, Jesus refers
to the Queen of Sheba as the Queen of the South, who will rise up to judge
the world at the last day. Her wisdom and judgement tie in well with the
function of the black Madonna as one who calls the soul to account for its
failings, and in the Song itself, the Beloved says, 'I am black but beautiful',
or, 'I am black *and* beautiful' (1.5) (the Hebrew text will yield either translation). These words are written in Latin over the statue of the black
Madonna at the Italian shrine of Tindari: *Nigra sum sed formosa*.

Now, the Hebrew word that is used here for black is *shechorah*, the feminine form of *shachar*. The etymology of this word relates it to the word for
dawn, and this association of words exists still in biblical texts, where the
word for the morning star is *ben-shachar*, that is, son of the dawn. The
Beloved gives as the reason for her dark colour the fact that she has been
working in the vineyard and is burnt by the sun; but the word's recollec-
tion of the dawn reminds the spiritual reader of the text that darkness
precedes light, so that, when read in relation to the Black Virgin, her
blackness is the darkness that comes before the daylight of Christ her son.
Here again, the Black Virgin is, amongst other things, a figure for spiritual
enlightenment.

The black Virgin of Paris, Notre-Dame de Bonne Délivrance, is traditionally attributed with the power to release prisoners from captivity.
Indeed, from the sixteenth to the eighteenth centuries, some of her devotees – members of a lay confraternity especially dedicated to her – would
collect money with which they would buy the release of captives in the
debtors' gaol in Paris.[16] From the time of Christ himself, freedom from
bondage to debt has been a powerful metaphor for liberation from bondage
to sin, and to anyone familiar with the Christian tradition, the charitable
acts of the black Virgin's devotees towards debtors resonates immediately
at the spiritual level. That the black Virgin desires to liberate men and
women not only from the darkness of the gaol and slavery to debt, but also
from spiritual darkness and imprisonment, is attested in a well-known

anecdote about St Francis de Sales (1567–1622). It is reported that, as a young man, he fell into the sin of despair – which nowadays, perhaps, we would call depression – and feared that he would not attain salvation. But he went to pray before the Black Virgin of Paris, and she heard his prayer and delivered him from his despair. From that time onwards, Francis never suffered again from that condition.[17]

The soul and the earth

Many twentieth-century writers on black Madonnas have noted that their blackness seems to be of spiritual importance, and have tried to fathom its precise significance, often by constructing elaborate theories of esoteric symbolism. These are the sorts of theories that are generally dismissed by 'respectable' academics as unscholarly and unworthy of serious considera-tion. Yet the fact that theories of this sort have a certain popularity suggests that they might tell us something about the spiritual condition of the age in which we live, and the student of religion would do well to pay them some attention. I shall therefore briefly describe one of the better researched and more stimulating of these theories, that of Jacques Bonvin.[18]

Bonvin takes up an existing hypothesis of spiritual energy in the land – something akin to the idea of ley lines – whereby there is supposed to be a grid of energy lines running under the earth's surface. At the points where the lines cross, the energy is disturbed, with the consequence that life at those points on the earth's surface is disrupted: crops will grow less well at these places, and animals and humans living there will be more than usu-ally subject to illness and other misfortune. Bonvin contends that in ancient and medieval times, although people would not have had a theory of an energy grid, they would nonetheless have perceived the special char-acter of these places of intersection, so that at the crossing points they erected monuments – megaliths or statues, for example – to perform a par-ticular function. That function was to channel the disturbed energy from beneath the earth's surface in such a way that it was not merely neut-ralized, but transformed into energy that would be healing and sacred. These places thus became shrines and places of pilgrimage.

According to Bonvin, the medieval black Virgins, such as those of Le Puy and Rocamadour, occupy sites of precisely this kind, and the function of the images is the transformation of energy from that which is harmful into that which is healing. Moreover, this transformation of spiritual energy in the earth corresponds to the process of spiritual enlightenment in the human person, by which we move from sin and ignorance to salvation and knowledge. The Virgin's blackness is the point at which our metamorphosis begins, and the Black Virgin has her counterpart in the White Virgin, who signifies the culmination of this process of transformation.

Bonvin believes that at the time when the black Virgin statues were sculpted, this path of spiritual enlightenment would have been available not merely to a select group of learned monks and nuns, but to the most ordinary men and women. He suggests that although the theories of spiritual transformation would have been known only to the orders of monks in whose churches these statues are often found, the use of these statues for popular devotion, alongside the other religious art, architecture and preaching of the period, would have meant that, by attending liturgies and praying before these images, ordinary worshippers would have been frequently exposed to symbols of spiritual transformation, and by this means brought to a state of enlightenment, even without having any precise language with which to describe their experience.

Now, whatever the accuracies or inaccuracies of Bonvin's telluric and historical hypotheses, his theory has some interesting points for consideration. First, let us notice his assumption that the human soul is formed in such a way as to correspond to the earth's energy, in its innate capacity to be moved from the bad to the good, understood as a movement from darkness to light. This correspondence recalls the theories of the human person as microcosm, which we have come across in a previous chapter. Morevoer, according to Bonvin, the Blessed Virgin is both a symbolic figure for the human soul and the energy of the earth in their respective stages of transformation, and also the agent of those processes of transformation.

Jacques Bonvin, I suggest, has correctly identified that there is a spiritual correspondence between the material creation and the human person, and that black Virgins embody the point of connection between them.

Mary as Chaos

If we take the correspondence between the human person and the cosmos to its most basic level, then the human soul is like the earth 'without form and void', with 'darkness on the face of the deep', over whom the Spirit of God hovers and whom the Lord calls into light. This is the imagery used in John's Gospel, when Nicodemus, on hearing that he must be 'born anew', asks, 'Can a man enter a second time into his mother's womb and be born?', and Christ replies, 'Truly, truly, I say to you, unless one is born of water and the Spirit, one cannot enter the Kingdom of God' (John 3.4–5). Water and the Spirit are active forces in the creation of the world, and Christ says that it is necessary to be recreated from one's very foundations. In normal Christian practice, entry into the Church, the body of Christ, is by baptism, which is rebirth by water and the Holy Spirit. On Easter Eve, at the Church's Easter Vigil ceremony, the waters of the font are blessed for baptisms in the coming year, and the font is presented as the 'womb' of the Church, from whom new Christians will be born. At the church of Kilpeck, in Herefordshire, there is an Anglo-Saxon font made in the shape of a pregnant belly, so that the symbol is quite unambiguous. Now, as we have already seen, it is because the Word of God became human in the womb of the Virgin Mary that it is possible for human beings to become united to him in the womb of the Church. The common English word for baptism is 'christening', that is, being 'Christ-ed', or made Christ; and it is as though in baptism the Christian is united to Christ in his conception in Mary's womb – a conception which is at the same time the renewal of the cosmos from its foundations – so that the baptized person, in their incorporation into Christ, is likewise entirely recreated. The waters of the deep at the dawn of creation are recapitulated in Mary's womb; and because of the work of her womb, those waters are again recapitulated in the womb of the Church, the baptismal font.

A number of writers on the subject of black Madonnas have suggested that the abiding significance of their blackness is the evocation of the primal darkness, the chaotic matter, or the earth that is 'without form and void', of which the universe is made. Emile Saillens suggests that this is the meaning of the blackness of both the black Virgins of Christianity and the black goddesses of other religious traditions, such as Kali in Hinduism.[19] If this is correct – at least with regard to Christianity – bearing in mind what has gone above with regard to the solidarity that exists amongst all things, then what is being said is that Mary in some way represents that in virtue of which things participate in one another by identity and out of which all new life is born. So let us ask what 'that' is.

First, we need to be precise about the nature of what I have called the 'elemental matrix' with which Mary is associated, and also about the character of that association. Some modern authors have suggested that Mary in some way signifies *prime matter*.[20] Let us consider first, then: what is the character of this 'prime matter'? For those philosophers and theologians who use the term, prime matter is the basic stuff of which the bodily (i.e., the 'physical', or non-spiritual) world is made. Theologians have had significant

differences of opinion as to its nature, but one thing that they agree on is
that the character of prime matter is, in at least one respect, mysterious.
This is because we can never perceive it with our bodily senses. Whenever
we perceive the material world with our ordinary senses, we experience
matter under some particular *form*. It may have the taste of strawberries,
the feel of rabbit fur, the sound of coughing, or the appearance of a scallop
shell; it may have the constantly shifting forms of the wind on a gusty day,
or daylight in a mountainous region; but one way or another, we never
come across matter in a formless state, and neither can we imagine such a
thing by recalling the experiences of our bodily senses. The matter of
things is not normally revealed to us *in itself*. Thomas Aquinas (1225–74),
whose philosophy has been highly influential in the modern period, followed Aristotle in holding that prime matter did not have any real existence in itself – that it is 'pure potentiality' until brought into existence by
some particular form. Others, however, such as Ramon Llull, had a
stronger doctrine of the character of matter. Llull, harking back to a more
ancient philosophy, taught that God made prime matter in a quantity that
remains always constant,[21] even though the forms that it takes vary widely.

The notion of the conservation of matter eventually found its way into
modern physics, where it came to be qualified when it was found that matter could be transformed into energy. For the physicist, therefore, it is the
quantity of matter and energy in the universe that remains constant. This
itself might suggest the basically ungraspable character of the nature of
matter. But however elusive the physical world turns out to be at levels
which scientists refer to as 'fundamental', the physicist will never
encounter prime matter; for however deeply physicists delve, it is only
under a form of some kind that they ever discover or examine matter and
energy. And this is necessarily the case, for our ordinary senses, and the
measuring tools that we make to extend the senses' power, cannot perceive
that which is formless. Deprivation of form is sensory deprivation. So this
all-pervasive substance of the material world – without which, forms likewise could not be perceived – cannot constitute the subject-matter of a
modern physical science. But this does not necessarily mean that prime
matter is nothing more than a useful hypothesis. When a body is buried in
earth where it is eaten by worms and gradually decays to become a constituent part of the soil in which it rests, or when a log is consumed by fire
and thus gives sustenance to the flame that devours it, we sense that a
transformation is taking place – that there is something which changes
from one form into another. And the term 'prime matter' refers to what

that 'something' ultimately is: that is to say, what it is at a level deeper than that at which our physical senses could ever know it. We can suppose matter without form to be a purely spiritual reality.

Now, to propose that there is a true correspondence between the Virgin Mary and prime matter is problematical. As we have seen, philosophers have not agreed as to whether it even has actual existence; and besides, its passive and inert character does not do justice to the dynamic nature of Mary's contribution to God's work of creation and redemption. So, rather than understanding Mary's association with the foundations of the cosmos by reference to prime matter, let us try thinking of Mary instead as having some sort of equivalence to 'Chaos'. The word 'chaos' is used by the Greek poet Hesiod, in his *Theogony*, written during the sixth century before Christ. Hesiod says that chaos was the first thing to arise, before the creation of any other thing.[22] From the point of view of the history of religious ideas, it seems likely that the biblical notion of 'the deep' (Hebrew: *tehom*) has antecedents in Ancient Near Eastern myths according to which the world was created out of the body of a sea-monster who signified 'chaos'. In Genesis 1.2, the Hebrew expression translated as 'without form, and void' is *tohu ve bohu*, from which English took the now obsolete phrase 'tohu bohu', meaning complete confusion, which is what is now commonly meant by the term 'chaos'. And within the Christian tradition, the mysterious figure of Chaos is described in detail by Ramon Llull, though not as something that is past and destroyed, but as an ever vital aspect of the physical world.

Llull's *Liber Chaos*, or *Book of Chaos*, was written as a commentary upon a diagram that appears in his *Demonstrative Art*.[23] The Art is a highly involved system of what might best be termed 'meditation exercises', whereby it is supposed to be possible to permutate the symbols of every quality or attribute in the world with the symbols of all the others in such a way as to find the true answer to any question. Llull believed that it had been given to him by God in a special revelation. It is important to understand the spiritual intent behind the Art, and consequently the *Book of Chaos*, because otherwise we might misunderstand the work on Chaos as a text that has the same sorts of concerns as modern science, which it does not. Llull's whole intention was that people should come to know and love God.[24] This is what humanity was originally created for, but one of the consequences of the Fall is that we have lost sight of this end. Llull believed that we could come once more to know and love God by means of knowing and loving God's creation. Knowing and loving are activities that cannot be separated: one cannot properly know something without loving it, and one cannot properly love something without knowing it. The *Book of Chaos* addresses the nature of the foundations of what we would call the 'physical' world, with a view to helping the enquirer, or meditator, to know that world so as to love it, and hence to come to know and love its Creator. So where the natural scientist might ask, 'What is this made of?' or 'How does this work?', either to gain knowledge for its own sake, or in order to be able to intervene in natural processes, Llull wants to know what is the nature of the world in relation to its Creator, for the sake of the world's salvation. Correspondingly, Llull approaches the world by means of prayer and meditation, rather than practical investigation.

Llull teaches that Chaos was made by God *ex nihilo* – 'out of nothing'. It is the foundation of all corporeal beings, and all that constitutes corporeal beings is initially present *potentially* in Chaos. That is to say, when a bodily object is perceived as the composition of its most fundamental constitutent parts, nothing is found there that does not already exist in Chaos. This includes human beings in our bodily aspect. (Each human soul, like other spiritual entities, is itself created by God *ex nihilo*.) Since everything in the corporeal, or bodily, world is composed of the four elements – fire, air, water and earth – the essences of these are present in Chaos. This means that both the form and the matter of the elements are present, as are all the other attributes and predicates (such as place and time) of the material cosmos. Llull says that not only 'prime matter', but also 'prime form' is present in Chaos; and although all the forms of all the elements are present in Chaos, Chaos as such is of one form. Now, all the constituent aspects of Chaos are confused in it. Because none of them has yet been made into a body – a distinct *something* – there is no corporeal fire to dry up water, nor any corporeal water to quench fire, and so the essences of the four elements, and all their attributes (heat, dryness, damp and cold) exist side by side. Difference, says Llull, is everywhere present in Chaos. The formation of individual bodies comes about by the relevant assembly of particular constituents and attributes under their appropriate forms. This is the process by which generation occurs, and the disintegration of these parts constitutes the process of decay.

It must be understood that Chaos is not something that existed only in the past, out of which things were once made; rather, it is always present, and exists in three stages. In its first stage, it is inchoate in the manner described above. Its second stage is the formation of the first forms, animal, vegetable and mineral – the first horse, the first tree, and so on; whilst its third stage is that of the new bodily beings that are made out of the first. This then gives rise to all subsequent stages down to the present. However, the first stage of Chaos, in which all things are potentially present, continues always to flow into the subsequent stages, so that, under its influence, bodily creatures can be formed in their progenitors without being exact copies of them. From this, we can say that *Chaos is that in virtue of which bodily things as such participate in one another by identity*.

So if we say that Mary in some way shares an identity with Chaos, is the figure of Mary a metaphor? Is her 'equivalence' to Chaos an imaginative device that merely signifies the scale of her importance in the work of redemption? Or is there some sense in which she actually participates in this matter of which the world is made? If Christ's conception in his mother's womb is truly a new creation – or rather, the re-creation of the world – from the foundations of the cosmos, then there must be some sense in which there is a true identity between Mary and Chaos. And by allowing the truth not only that bodies in general can participate in one another by identity, but that all bodies participate in Chaos, we can see that, just as the incarnation of the Word of God in Christ entails a union with the whole of the physical creation, and just as his taking flesh in Mary is a participation in the foundations of that creation, so Mary herself shares an identity with those very foundations, that is, with Chaos.

Now, it may be pointed out that, on this argument, Mary's relationship to Chaos is no different from anyone else's, since we all share in this participation of one in all and all in one. And this is partly true. All earthly creatures participate in Chaos and share a measure of common being because of this. However, Mary's relationship to matter also has a character that is unique. For most of us, our participation in Chaos occurs simply in virtue of our being corporeal beings. For Mary, however, the purpose of the incarnation of God in her body was precisely the union of God with the whole cosmos; so the participation of Mary in the fabric of the universe is not just a necessary aspect of her humanity, but is essential to the world's redemption and to the fulfilment of its purpose. And this is why it is she in particular who shares an identity with the fundamental substance of the physical world. Indeed, to grasp properly the mystery of the Incarnation, we need to keep perceiving this identity of Mary with the world's foundations over and over again. In this, as in all other teachings about Mary, she is both representative of something that is true of all earthly beings, and at the same time unique.

However, in being not only the place and the instrument, but also the human person, by whom God binds the creation to himself, Mary participates in the spiritual as well as the physical creation. Indeed, Christian tradition maintains that her place in heaven is higher even than that of the angels; that, after Christ in his humanity, she is the most excellent of created spiritual beings. Mary as microcosm encompasses the most ethereal heights of the spiritual world and the most opaque depths of the material. It is thus that a shrine of the Virgin in the darkness of a woodland thicket or a cave may simultaneously be a place of spiritual illumination, and for this reason we can learn to see the union of spirit and matter in the place where God makes Godself present: that is, everywhere.

Yet to speak of Chaos in terms of spiritual excellence seems strange, for is 'chaos' not usually a term employed to designate a state that is undesirable? Do we not think of 'order' as its nobler antithesis? Well, part of the genius of Llull's conception of Chaos is his rescuing of the concept from connotations of evil. In some ancient mythologies, the world is created as a result of a battle between a god and a chaos monster, in which the chaos monster is defeated. For some Christian theologians, chaos is even more thoroughly eradicated, since it is never present at all in God's creation: all things are ordered, by form being appropriately imposed upon matter, from the beginning. Llull, however, sees the confusion that is Chaos as being the first act of God's creative power, all subsequent order being potentially present within it. The historian Frances Yates, commenting upon Llull's conception of Chaos, sees it as having a Godlike quality. It is closest to God in the sense that it comes from him first, before anything else is created; moreover, it does not have the separation and individuation which characterize the later creation and which make that later creation quite different from the unboundedness of its divine maker. With regard to Llull's conception of Chaos, Yates writes: 'Its formlessness is not the disorder of evil, but near to the divine informity [i.e., unformed state].'[25] So the human perfection of the Blessed Virgin Mary corresponds to the heavenly character of the foundations of the material world.

Yet Yates' observation is not without its difficulty, for we have already seen that, according to Llull, *difference* is everywhere in Chaos, although in God, who is perfect unity, difference does not exist. But perhaps this sort of ambivalence is inherent to the condition of Chaos. The first stage of Chaos is the creation in its least perfected state. It has to be made into elements, minerals, plants, animals and humans. And when it is made into human beings, it has a unique degree of intimacy with the purely spiritual world of the angels and heaven. According to Llull, all this was done in order that God might become incarnate in one man, Jesus of Nazareth, and thereby – since the human person is a micrososm – bring the whole universe to completion. So Chaos has a twofold status: on the one hand, it is that in creation which, in its basic state, is farthest from perfection; yet on the other hand, it comes immediately from the hand of God, and has Godlike aspects that are proper to it alone.

Perhaps a similar sort of ambiguity inheres in the blackness of black Virgins – images of exceptional sanctity, yet painted in the colour that Europeans have associated, since at least the Middle Ages, with inferiority and evil. The statue of Our Lady of Le Puy was outstandingly sacred, being believed to have been carved by the prophet Jeremiah. Yet it was treasured in Babylon, the city of Israel's captivity, proverbial for all that is ungodly. And in the later version of the legend, according to which the image was recovered during the Crusades, it was Moors who actively fought against Christians who were the statue's guardians and protectors.

The chaos of the earth

In a highly illuminating study of the cultural significance of woodlands for human civilization, the literary scholar, Robert Pogue Harrison, draws attention to the association that exists between civilization's perception of forests and its idea of untamed nature, or 'chaos', and, in particular, to the frightening character of the wildwood in the eyes of city-dwellers.[26] This frightening aspect of the natural world may be quite close to the surface in the cults of many black Madonnas. The anthropologists Leonard Moss and Stephen Cappanari made a study of the cults of black Madonnas in southern Italy, from which they argued that the cults of these Madonnas supersede those of pagan goddesses of fertility, and that the significance of their blackness is that black is the colour of fertile earth. Black Madonnas, they suggest, are protectresses of the fertility of the soil and share their colour with that soil.[27] But soil has ambiguous connotations. For on the one hand, it is a source of life, the giver of plants and therefore of sustenance for both animals and humans, but on the other hand, it is where the dead are buried and decay. Soil gives rise to the bodies of new life, but also consumes the bodies of the lifeless. Some black Madonnas are attributed with the special power of granting fertility – Our Lady of Montserrat, in Catalonia, for example – whilst others have presided over burial places – Notre-Dame de Ronzières, in Auvergne, for instance, or Notre-Dame de Bonne Mort, in Clermont Cathedral.

Harrison argues that it is forests which constitute the archetypal places of birth and decay. By looking at the mythology and philosophy of urban peoples, he suggests that human beings see the forest as the place of our origins: in both antiquity and modernity, men and women have believed that we are descended from forest dwellers. Yet civilization has consisted of the progressive movement away from these origins. It has entailed the cutting down of woodland and a fear of the darkness of tree cover. In the forest, nature is in a state of confusion and disorder, unlike the city, in which all is supposed to be under human control. This silvan confusion of forms and colours, flora and fauna, is the matrix from which all life comes and to which it returns. But civilization tries to cut itself off from its origins and to deny its mortality, and so fears the wildwood.[28]

Harrison takes the view that the whole panoply of the natural processes governing human life was once regarded as sacred and personified as a goddess, or goddesses. The confusion apparently inherent in soil and woods was the divine womb that gave life and received it back in death. The Latin word *mater*, meaning 'mother', seems to have a common root with *materia*, meaning 'matter', and in Harrison's reconstruction of cultural history, the goddess's womb was the matrix or chaotic matter from which all things are formed and into which they ultimately disintegrate. It was only at a later time that human society tried to break away from this source of its existence, and from the divine mother. But many ordinary people were unwilling to make this break from the goddess, and this, Harrison suggests, was a strong motive force behind the development of the cult of the Virgin Mary in Christianity.[29]

Whether there is or is not an association between the cult of the Virgin and earlier pagan practices, we can note that a number of shrines of the Virgin, including those of black Madonnas, do have woodland origins. The cult at Le Puy-en-Velay has already been cited. In Switzerland, the largest pilgrim shrine is that of Our Lady of Einsiedeln, whose foundation legend recounts that the shrine had its origin in a remote woodland hermitage inhabited by a holy man, St Meinrad.[30] Likewise, the once popular shrine of Our Lady of Willesden, now in north London, is said to have begun as the oratory of a small group of monks in the middle of what was then the Middlesex woods. The mythology of the Willesden shrine has other explicit connections with the natural world. There is a healing spring by the church, and in the churchyard there was once an oak tree where the Virgin appeared in a vision to a pilgrim.

Other black Virgin shrines are located in places that are wild, although not especially forested. Rocamadour, for instance, is on a ledge of a cliff face of the limestone gorge cut by the River Alzou, as it flows through the barren plateau of the Causse de Quercy which rises up between the valleys of the Lot and the Dordogne. Montserrat is also a rock shrine, high on the curiously formed Sierra de Montserrat.

It is as though the irregularity and confusion of forms in the wilderness provide us with a sense not only of our immediate earthly origins, but of the origins of the cosmos itself. And when we are wise and trusting, we can see the divine foundation of all these things – of ourselves, of the wilderness and of the entire universe – and honour them for their special association with Mary, who pervades the fruitfulness of Chaos.

Separation and ambiguity

Reflecting upon the nature of the city, Robert Pogue Harrison writes:

> Walls, no less than writing, define civilization. They are monuments against time, like writing itself … . Walls protect, divide, distinguish; above all, they *abstract*. The basic activities that sustain life – agriculture and stock breeding, for instance – take place beyond the walls. Within the walls one is within an emporium; one is within the jurisdiction of a bureaucracy; one is within the abstract identity of race, city, and institutionalized religion … . [These are] walls that divide history from prehistory, culture from nature, sky from earth, life from death, memory from oblivion.[31]

The abstraction of which Harrison writes began in antiquity, but has now become so sophisticated that city walls are no longer necessary to maintain it. The walls of a house in remote countryside can provide even greater separation from 'the basic activities that sustain life' if the inhabitants of the house can travel within the walls of an air-conditioned car to a supermarket, within whose walls food from across the world can be acquired, ready-made or ready-cleaned, in polythene wrapping. And when they return home, our shoppers can sit amongst building materials and fabrics that are so highly processed that only a chemical engineer could tell you what natural substances constitute their base materials.

On Harrison's understanding, exclusion and separation is in the nature (so to speak) of civilization, yet is also a mistake, because it is deceitful. For as a matter of fact, we are – at least in part – material beings who do depend upon natural processes for our existence. And a striking feature of many Marian shrines is the force with which they call people back to the source of our physical life by making them cross over that boundary that divides 'culture from nature'. A common legend of the origin of a shrine is one which tells that a statue of the Virgin was found by an animal, usually a bull or an ox, in a bush or a spring. The herdsman sees the animal pawing at the ground, and when he goes to find out why, he sees that it has discovered the holy image. He runs off to the village to tell what has happened, and the people come out and take the statue into the village in a grand procession, culminating in the statue being set up in a place of honour in the parish church. The next morning, however (as we have seen in the case of El Rocío), the statue has disappeared, and has miraculously returned to the spot on which it was found. Typically, the legend says that the people return the image to the village once or twice more, but each time, the statue returned to its original site. From this, the people understand that Our Lady wished to be honoured in the place of her own choosing. So a shrine is constructed to house the image with the bush or the spring where it was discovered, and the Virgin's devotees must make a pilgrimage away from the world of their own artifice to a site where 'the basic activities that sustain life' take place.

At some shrines, the cult is quite explicitly tied to those basic activities. The Catalan shrine of Our Lady of Núria, for example, is situated in a high mountain valley where shepherds used to graze their flocks in the summer months of July and August, and the chapel there is said to have been founded by St Gil, who brought the gospel to the shepherds and who lived there as their spiritual guide.[32]

Our Lady of Vassivière, in the diocese of Clermont, is also associated with the summer pasturing of flocks. In her case, however, the cult statue is taken in procession to the shrine in the meadows at Vassivière at the beginning of the summer period, and in September is ceremonially returned to her winter home in the nearby town of Besse-en-Chandesse.

With modern means of communication – the walled-in spaces of trains, planes and cars – places that were once remote, so that even the fittest pilgrim was brought face-to-face with his or her physical frailty, can often be reached with relative ease. Yet, since human beings in truth are just as material and just as vulnerable as we have always been, this separation from physical necessity means that the danger of our being deluded by our own cleverness is greater than ever. We therefore urgently need to perceive our dependence upon natural processes, and, through them, upon the God who is the source of our life and to whom we shall return at the end of that life. We need to know and to love the Chaos from which we try to separate ourselves, and to know it as made by, and beloved of, God. This, amongst other things, is what the black Virgin summons us to do.

There is a further point that needs to be made here. We have been considering civilization as based upon acts of separation and division, and in particular, upon an actual and pretended separation of city dwellers from natural processes. We have also seen that there is an ambiguity about humanity's relationship with these processes, since however much we try to distance ourselves from them, they remain the source and substance of our material existence. We should therefore take account of the fact that, in human culture, the significance of actions and objects that are set apart from everyday life is likewise sometimes ambiguous.

We can find an example of this in the biblical book of Joshua, where we read that, when the Hebrew tribes invade the land of Canaan, the Lord imposes a *cherem* upon many of the possessions of the Canaanites. The word *cherem* is usually translated as 'ban'. It means that the things which belonged to the Canaanites are forbidden to the Hebrews; this is because they are especially devoted to the Lord. Indeed, the notion of 'that which is devoted to sacred use' is one aspect of the concept of *cherem*, and some objects within the area of the *cherem* – namely, vessels made of precious metals – are sacred to the Lord in such a way that they are to be preserved in the Lord's treasury (Joshua 6.19). Other objects, however, are devoted to the Lord specifically for the purpose of destruction (e.g. Joshua 6.17). On the other hand, those Israelites who break faith with the *cherem* by taking objects for themselves render themselves under the *cherem*, in the sense that they too are given over to destruction (Joshua 7.12), with no suggestion that they, having breached the sacred code, are in any way consecrated. *Cherem* means something not unlike *tabu*, that is, set apart from everyday use *either* because of exceptional holiness *or* because of exceptional unholiness.

A well-nigh universal practice of separation in human society is that by which women are forbidden to enter certain places or undertake certain activities during their menstrual bleeding. This too can be ambiguous in its meaning. Is the separation imposed because menstruation is regarded as exceptionally nasty or as exceptionally sacred? It is common to assume the former, but the situation is rarely as clear as this. Paula Weidegger carried out a study of menstrual rites in various cultures of the world, and included in her research a survey of women in the United States. Reporting on these, she writes:

Among Jewish families, ... it is customary to slap a young woman's face on the day that menstruation begins. The women I have met who had this experience say they hadn't the vaguest notion of why their mothers slapped them. Many believed that it was a unique experience and the product of an aberration or a disturbed mother. Only one woman reported a different experience. She had a sense of tradition and posititve feelings about her first menstruation. Her mother had taken her into the living room, and said, 'As my mother did to me, as her mother did to her, so I do to you today.' The mother then slapped her daughter across the face. When this woman grew up she said she felt proud to be menstruating and enjoyed a feeling of connection with her female ancestors – it gave her a sense of generational continuity which she, in turn, passed on to her daughter.[33]

The demarcation of a menstruating woman is here a cause for honour, not shame.

Now, although the separation of cities from their natural surroundings has undoubtedly been connected to a hatred of natural processes, the power and fear which engender that hatred may also have engendered a sense of reverence. Indeed, the frequency with which the ever-popular Virgin Mary has her favoured shrines in wilderness locations suggests that a sense of the holiness of the wild continued to flourish long after the time at which urban culture began to have a major influence upon human society. Here again, then, the act of separation may have a double meaning.

At its most fundamental level, this ambiguity can be seen in the account of Chaos given above. We have seen that the first stage of Chaos is, on the one hand, that which is closest to God and is in a strong sense Godlike, yet, on the other hand, is that which, being the lowest rung on the ladder of creation and thus furthest from creation's final destiny, is most distant from God. And this Chaos is present in all things, yet at the same time is more radically set apart than anything else in creation, since it can never be perceived or known by us with our bodily senses.

John Scotus Erigena, the great Irish theologian of the ninth century, touches on this ambiguity with regard to *matter*. His cosmogony does not include the Chaos of Llull, but he pays considerable attention to the prime matter of which the world is made. John's theology is extremely deep and subtle, and I shall not presume to try to give any kind of adequate representation of it. But it may be only a theology as deep and subtle as his that can lead us, at an intellectual level, to see the meaning of the Virgin's blackness, and at the same time to see our way out of the present muddle of wrong relationships in which the world is entangled, so that we can progress to the clarity of a sacred perception of things; and for this reason, I introduce a glimpse of John's ideas at a point at which only his words say precisely what needs to be said.

Erigena says that the first stage of creation 'is spoken of by Scripture as formless matter: matter because it is the beginning of the essence of things; formless because it comes nearest to the formlessness of the divine Wisdom',[34] who is the Word. Yet the similarity that exists between God and matter should not lead us to identify one with the other: quite the contrary. Erigena writes:

> ... there are two, and only two, that cannot be defined, God and matter. For God is without limit and without form since He is formed by none, being the Form of all things. Similarly matter is without form and without limit, for it needs to be formed and limited from elsewhere, while in itself it is not form but something that can receive form. And this similarity between the Cause of all things ... and this unformed cause – I mean matter – which was created to the end that those things which in themselves cannot be grasped by the senses might by some means have a sensible appearance in it, is understood in contrary sense.[35]

God is formless and inconceivable because God is *above* and *before* every form; whilst matter is formless and inconceivable because it *awaits the reception* of form. The similarity between God and matter thus goes hand in hand with the most radical dissimilarity between the two. But if we consider either the likeness or the difference without the other, then we fail to sense the mysteriousness of the relationship that exists between the subjects God and matter.

Erigena considers another ambiguity when he examines the statement that God is 'Nothing'. Since God is the true being of all things, it seems strange to designate God in this way, yet, Erigena contends, it is not wrong to do so. The reason why God can be referred to as 'Nothing' is that God is above any formed thing that exists within creation or that the human mind can form a concept of. 'Nothing' refers to 'the ineffable and incomprehensible and inaccessible brilliance of the divine Goodness', who is the Word. The work of creation is the descent of the divine Goodness into created things: 'that which is properly thought of as beyond all essence is also properly known in all essence, and therefore every visible and invisible creature can be called a theophany, that is, a divine apparition.' The more intimately a nature (either divine or created) is understood, 'the closer it is seen to approach the divine brilliance'. This brilliance is often called 'darkness', because it cannot be comprehended.[36]

So that which is furthest from God is simultaneously that which is closest to God; at the heart of the humblest of creatures is nothing other than the divine Goodness; and darkness is a cipher for light. Seen in this way, the blackness of the Black Madonna may refer precisely to these paradoxes.

Notes

1 For accounts of the shrine of Our Lady of Le Puy, see Paul, G. and P., *Notre-Dame du Puy: Essai historique et archéologique*, Cazes-Bonneton, Le Puy-en-Velay, 1950; Begg, E., *The Cult of the Black Virgin*, Penguin (Arkana), London, 1996, 212–14; Saillens, E., *Nos Vierges Noires: Leurs origines*, Les Editions Universelles, Paris, 1945, 84–95; Gostling, F.M., *Auvergne and its People*, Methuen, London, 1911, 162–79.

2 Gostling, *op. cit.*, 165.

3 *La fondacion de la saincte eglise & singulier oratoire de nostre dame du puy* [copy in British Library has lost page containing printer's details, but date in catalogue is given as 1500].

4 A good and well-illustrated discussion of the image is given in Kaeppelin, P., 'La Sainte Image de Notre-Dame du Puy', *Le fil de la Borne*, 22, Centre del'Etude de la Vallée de la Borne, Bains, 1997.

5 Vilatte, S., 'La Question des "Vierges Noires"', in *La Vierge à l'Epoque Romane: Culte et représentations*, that is, *Revue d'Auvergne*, 542, Société des Amis des Universités de Clermont-Ferrand, Clermont-Ferrand, 1997, 12–38, at 13. Mary Elizabeth Perry claims that Mary is sometimes represented as black in Spanish illuminated manuscripts from the eighth century onwards ('The Black Madonna of Montserrat', in Richardson Keller, F. (ed.), *Views of Women's Lives in Western Tradition*, Edwin Mellen Press, Lampeter, 1990, 109–28, at 116, citing evidence from Delclaux, F., *Imàgenes de la Virgen en los Codices Medievales de España*, Patronato Nacional de Museos, Madrid, 1973.

6 For Italian examples, see Birnbaum, L.C., *Black Madonnas: Feminism, Religion, and Politics in Italy*, Northeastern University Press, Boston, 1993.

7 A very important study that takes account of a certain number of figures from outside France is Durand-Lefebvre, M., *Etude sur l'Origine des Vierges Noires*, G. Durassié, Paris, 1937.

8 Cassagnes-Brouquet, S., *Vierges Noires: Regard et fascination*, Editions du Rouergue, Rodez, 1990.

9 Saillens, *op. cit.*

10 Cassagnes-Brouquet, *op. cit.*, 150–9.

11 Vilatte, *op. cit.*

12 *The Mabingion* (trans. G. and J. Jones), Dent, London and New York, [Everyman's Library], 1949, 183–227.

13 *The Mabinogion*, 192.

14 *The Mabinogion*, 214–17.

15 *The Mabinogion*, 218.

16 De Bascher, J., *La Vierge Noire de Paris*, Téqui, Paris, 1979, 70–3.

17 Vincent, F., 'Saint François de Sales', in du Manoir, H. (ed.), *Maria: Etudes sur la Sainte Vierge*, II, Beauchesne, Paris, 1952, 991–1004, at 995–6.

18 Bonvin, J., *Vierges Noires: La réponse vient de la terre*, Dervy, Paris, 1988.

19 Saillens, *op. cit.*, 238–44.

20 See Boss, S. J., *Empress and Handmaid: On Nature and Gender in the Cult of the Virgin Mary*, Cassell, London, 2000, 115 n.50.

21 Llull, R., 'Libre de Contemplació' 31.3, in *Obres Essencials*, Vol. 1, Edicions Ariel, Barcelona, 1957, 164.

22 'The Theogony of Hesiod', 116, in *Hesiod: The Homeric Hymns and Homerica* (Greek text with trans. by H.G. Evelyn-White), Heinemann, [Loeb Classical Library], London, 1982, 86–7.

23 Lullius, R., 'Liber Chaos', in *Operum*, tom. III., Häffner, Mainz, 1723.

24 Vega, A., *Rámon Llull y el Secreto de la Vida*, 52, 58 and *passim*.

25 Yates, F. A., 'Rámon Lull and John Scotus Erigena', in *Lull & Bruno: Collected Essays*, Vol. 1., Routledge and Kegan Paul, London, 1982, 78–125, at 96.

26 Harrison, R. P., *Forests: The Shadow of Civilization*, University of Chicago Press, Chicago, 1992.

27 Moss, L. W., and Cappanari, S. C., 'In Quest of the Black Virgin: She is black because she is black', in Preston, J. J. (ed.), *Mother Worship: Themes and Variations*, University of North Carolina Press, Chapel Hill, North Carolina, 1982, 53–74.

28 Harrison, *op. cit.*, 1–58.

29 Harrison, *op. cit.*, 21.

30 Gustafson, F., *The Black Madonna*, Sigo Press, Boston, Massachusetts, 1990, 1–19.

31 Harrison, *op. cit.*, 14–15.

32 Herce, A.H., *Vall de Núria: Libro guía*, FGC/Vall de Núria, Barcelona, 2001, 11–21.

33 Weidegger, P., *Female Cycles*, The Women's Press, London, 1978, 163–4.

34 Eriugena, I.S., *Periphyseon (De Divisione Naturae)*, Vol. III, Sheldon-Williams, I.P. (ed.), Dublin Institute for Advanced Studies, Dublin, 1981, 168–9.

35 Eriugena, I.S., *Periphyseon (De Divisione Naturae)* Vol. I, Sheldon-Williams, I.P. (ed.), Dublin Institute for Advanced Studies, Dublin, 1968, 166–7.

36 Eriugena, I.S., *Periphyseon (De Divisione Naturae)* Vol. III, Sheldon-Williams, I.P. (ed.), Dublin Institute for Advanced Studies, Dublin, 1981, 166–7.

7

Godlike Virginity

A sense that the relationship between Mary and her son is the created likeness of the relationship between the persons of the Trinity is implicit not
only in the Christian understanding of Mary's motherhood, but also of her
virginity. The teachings concerning Mary's virginity, however, are probably
the Marian doctrines that seem most puzzling or problematical to contemporary men and women. We have already seen that Mary was a virgin
when she conceived Christ. But the dominant traditions of Christianity
(the Roman Catholic, Eastern Orthodox, older churches such as the
Coptic, as well as several important Protestant reformers) have held to the
view that she also remained a virgin throughout her life, and, moreover,
that her body remained physically unchanged during childbirth.

The doctrine of Mary's perpetual virginity states that she remained a
virgin before, during and after the birth of Christ and a number of modern
writers have found difficulty in particular with belief in the *in partu*
virginity, that is, virginity during parturition. This doctrine is first found
in texts which probably date from the second century AD, including the
Protevangelium of James, and became normal Christian teaching within a
few centuries. Part of the purpose of the doctrine is to show that Christ is
truly divine: the fact that he had a human mother shows he is human; but
his miraculous birth shows he is also God. Furthermore, Mary's miraculous childbirth constitutes the beginning of the restoration of Paradise.
When God expelled Adam and Eve from Eden, life for the man and the
woman became hard – but perhaps harder for her than for him, since his
lordship over her was one of the consequences of the expulsion. For Adam,
the main penalty was the need to labour to eke out a living from the earth;
whilst for Eve, it was the suffering of pain in childbirth (Genesis 3.16–19).
So when God became incarnate in a human baby, to redeem the world from
the consequences of the Fall and prepare it to attain its proper glory, the
danger and sickness of childbirth were done away within his very birth.
Since Christ became human in order to take away the world's sin, it was
right that he should enter the world in such a way that the woman who

gave birth to him in his humanity would not by that action suffer any consequence of human sin. In her childbearing, she already embodies the promise of redemption.

At various times in the history of Christianity, theologians have been concerned that the idea of the *in partu* virginity in effect undermines belief in Christ's full humanity. In the twentieth century, the Catholic theologian Karl Rahner suggested that the doctrine needed to be reinterpreted as referring to Mary's spiritual and mental, rather than physical, condition, on the grounds that it was 'too mythical' for modern people to be able to accept as referring directly to a physical event. Some feminist authors have been concerned that Mary's miraculous childbearing makes her too far removed from the condition of ordinary women, and that it thereby suggests that normal womanhood is in some way lacking and unacceptable to God. Against these criticisms, I have argued elsewhere that within Christian tradition there exists a rich variety of ways of interpreting Mary's virginity, and in particular, that this doctrine has been attractive to women in childbirth because it offers hope that Mary, who has given birth without pain or injury, may be able to assist them also to obtain a safe delivery.[1] Here, however, I am pursuing a different line of enquiry, because there seems to be a deeper level of symbolic meaning behind the doctrine of Mary's perpetual virginity, and it is this which I hope to draw out.

Within the multiplicity of creation, acts of generation and fruitfulness always involve the breaching of boundaries. Seeds break out of the walls of fruit, chicks break open their eggs, and cows struggle to push calves from inside their bellies to the outside world. All these processes are acts of change which leave ruptures and scars on the organs that bear that change. In God, however, there is generation and procession that does not entail any rupture, or the crossing of a boundary. This is what is said in the human attempt to understand the one God as Trinity. For God is one, with no division and no boundary or limit of any kind. There is no 'end' to God, so there is no 'outside' of God, and consequently no 'inside' either. And there are no 'parts' of God: God is not made up, or composed, of lesser units, such as atoms, or bodily organs. God is infinite and eternal unity. So although the first person of the Trinity, the Father, begets the Son, this begetting does not involve passing over any limit, as happens, say, in human begetting, where the boundaries of both a male and a female body are breached. Neither, indeed, is this a process of change. For change is to do with the way things are 'afterwards', as compared with how they were 'before', that is, it is a function of *time*; but the generation of the

Word takes place in eternity – that is, outside time. Likewise, the Holy Spirit proceeds from the Father and the Son in an act that is changeless and eternal. Yet paradoxically, the Word of God is born in time, as a human creature from his mother Mary, and in being born, he passes from inside her womb to the outside world. Generations of mystical visionaries have reiterated that we do not know how this was accomplished – only that, after the birth, Mary's body was unchanged from the state it was in before conception. Thus, for example, the influential visionary, St Bridget of Sweden (c.1303–73) – herself a mother of several children – gives a detailed account of a vision she had of Christ's birth, in which she saw the Virgin kneeling in ecstasy, and,

> while [the Virgin] was thus in prayer, I saw the One lying in her womb then move; and then and there, in a moment and the twinkling of an eye, she gave birth to a Son, from whom there went out such great and ineffable light and splendor that the sun could not be compared to it. ... And so sudden and momentary was that manner of giving birth that I was unable to notice or discern how or in what member she was giving birth.[2]

Some authors maintained that Christ was born not from Mary's womb but from some other organ of her body. St Hildegard, who also wrote about childbirth, midwifery and women's ailments, was of this opinion:

> When the blessed Virgin was a little weakened, as if drowsy with sleep, the infant came forth from her side – not from the opening of the womb – without her knowledge and without pain, corruption, or filth, just as Eve emerged from the side of Adam.[3]

Hildegard here presents Christ and Mary as the Second Adam and Eve, in whom humanity is restored to its original glory. This theme is common in Catholic writing, although not usually connected to the idea that Christ was born from Mary's side. More commonly it has been taught that, although Mary gave birth miraculously, she did so from the womb. How this apparent impossibility could be the case was discussed in great detail by medieval and Renaissance theologians.

Durandus (c.1237–96), Bishop of Mende, argued that if Adam and Eve had not fallen from grace, then Eve would have given birth without any physical injury or pain, and Mary's childbearing was as Eve's would have been had Adam not sinned. Durandus suggested that in a parturition of this ideal kind, the mother's bodily organs would contract sufficiently to make way for the passage of the infant out of the mother's body without causing her any pain or wounding. The woman's body would then return to its former condition unharmed.

This refusal to allow any change to Mary's body in childbirth takes a particularly extreme form in the mariology of Francisco Suárez, who rejects even the version given by Durandus, in insisting that, by some incomprehensible miracle, the birth of Christ would have made no difference whatsoever to the organs of Mary's body. The reason he gives for holding this view is that if Mary had undergone any bodily change, then this would have compromised her virginity. It is as though, for Suárez, Mary's virginity is a state of changelessness that is the earthly counterpart to the changelessness of the Persons of the Blessed Trinity.

I suggest that part of the meaning of Mary's perpetual virginity is that, in the birth of Christ from his mother, not only is Paradise restored, but heaven – the immediate presence of the Blessed Trinity – is revealed as a condition that is possible on earth. To bear in mind that the relationship between Christ and Mary is an image of the Blessed Trinity gives us an insight into the meaning of Mary's virginity in childbirth; for just as the Son proceeds from the Father, and the Holy Spirit from Father and Son, in the way in which light proceeds from light – that is, without any alteration in the flame that is the source – so Christ is born of Mary without any material breach in her body. In her virginal motherhood, Mary manifests to the fullest possible extent the generating action of the God whose Son is also her own.

Notes

1 Boss, S.J., *Empress and Handmaid: On Nature and Gender in the Cult of the Virgin Mary*, Cassell, London, 2000, 64–6 and 187–96.

2 'Seventh Book of Revelations, 21.8, 10', in *Birgitta of Sweden: Life and Selected Revelations* (trans. A. R. Kezel), Paulist Press, New York and Mahwah [Classics of Western Spirituality series], 1990, 203.

3 Fragment IV.6–7, in Schipperges, H. (ed.), 'Ein unveröffentlichtes Hildegard-Fragment', *Sudhoffs Archiv für Geschischte de Medizin* 40 (1956), 41–77, at 68; quoted in English in Newman, B., *Sister of Wisdom: St. Hildegard's Theology of the Feminine*, Scholar Press, Aldershot, 1987, 176. Newman also discusses Hildegard's writing on women's physical health in *Sister of Wisdom*, 121–55.

8
Wisdom and Sovereignty

In the Old Testament Scriptures, the work of creation is closely associated with Holy Wisdom, and in Catholic tradition, the figure of Wisdom is associated with the Virgin Mary. A study of Mary in relation to creation therefore demands a consideration of Wisdom. Visual images have always been central to the cult of the Virgin, and I begin this consideration of Mary and Wisdom by examining one of the most important Marian images, the so-called 'Seat of Wisdom'.

The visit of the Magi

Every year at Christmas time, many Christians send greetings cards depicting the Adoration of the Magi – the visit of the three wise men, or kings, to the infant Jesus. Often these cards show Renaissance paintings from the fifteenth or sixteenth centuries, but the motif of the Adoration is one of the most ancient in Christian art. It appears in the Catacombs in Rome, probably painted in the third century, being an image that is taken in the first instance from the Gospels. The visitation of the Magi to the infant Jesus is recorded in Matthew 2.11: 'and going into the house [where the child was], the Magi saw the child with Mary his mother, and they fell down and worshipped him.'

The Gospel text does not tell us anything about Mary's posture or demeanour at the time of the visit, but in ancient and medieval art, she is always enthroned and has a regal bearing, with her son seated on her lap. In fact, this is not out of keeping with the narrative of Matthew's Gospel, which begins with Christ's genealogy in which King David is identified as one of Jesus' ancestors. Matthew clearly does want the reader to understand that Jesus is descended from the royal line of David, of the house of Judah. Indeed, it is possible that the reference to Mary in this verse (Mattthew 2.11) is intended to be a reference to the office of Queen Mother, which seems to have been held by the mothers of the kings of Judah. But from the earliest Christianity, Jesus' kingship was associated not only with

Figure 3. Virgin in Majesty of Clermont Cathedral,
Bibilothèque Municipale de Clermont, ms 145 (reproduced in Pourreyon, C.,
Le Culte de Notre-Dame au Diocèse de Clermont en Auvergne, Editions F. Bost,
Nancy, 1936; and in Laurentin, R., and Oursel, R., *Vierges Romanes*,
Zodiaque, La Pierre-qui-Vire, 1988)

that of the royal line of Judah, but, more importantly, with the governance of the universe – of the whole created order, moral and physical. So the three kings are earthly rulers who have come to do homage to the Lord, under whose authority all temporal rulers hold their respective offices.

During the seventh and eighth centuries, it became common to represent the Virgin and Child in the same posture of enthronement in which they are shown in Adoration scenes, but without the magi. Mosaics of this kind exist in Rome and Constantinople, and, stripped now of the narrative element of the Visitation, form a clear focal point for devotion. From the tenth century, starting in the Auvergne region of France, images of this kind began to be made as free-standing statues. A statue of this kind is known as a Virgin in Majesty, or Seat of Wisdom, and the iconography of the Seat of Wisdom is the subject of the first section of this chapter.

The iconography of the Incarnation

The earliest recorded free-standing statue of the Virgin Mary was made in 946 for the cathedral at Clermont (now Clermont-Ferrand) in southeastern central France. The statue is depicted in a manuscript written by Arnold the Deacon (Figure 3).[1] Arnold recounts how, after the cathedral had been destroyed by Norman invaders, Bishop Etienne II had it rebuilt and commissioned a statue of the Virgin and Child to stand over the main altar. The statue was made by Aleaume, the cathedral architect, who was also a goldsmith, and it contained relics of Christ and Our Lady. The picture shows a statue made according to a model that continued to be used by artists who carved other, wooden, statues which still exist, both in Auvergne and elsewhere, and that is also seen in flat representations, such as manuscript illumination. Christ is shown here not as an infant, but as a child with rather adult features. Behind his head there is a cruciform halo, and his right hand is raised in blessing. He bears a cross in his left hand, and his feet are bare. His mother Mary is enthroned, with one hand around her son's chest, and the other extended so that it curls slightly around in front of him. Similar iconography can be seen in an illuminated manuscript from Eynsham Abbey, Oxfordshire, in which Christ's left hand holds a book (Figure 4), and on the fifteenth-century seal of Walsingham Priory, showing the statue of Our Lady of Walsingham.

It seems very likely that Majesty statues were influenced by older pagan images, but, as we have seen, this type of iconography is found in representations of the Adoration of the Magi, and it is certainly the Adoration

Figure 4. Seat of Wisdom (c.1130–1140). Manuscript of Augustine's *Commentary on Psalms 101–150*, probably from Eynsham Abbey. Bodleian Library, Oxford

that is the principal Christian source for these figures. So the statue is, as it were, taken out of the context of the visit of the magi. The word 'magi' is the plural of 'magus', from which we get the word 'magic'. Magical powers, like wisdom, can be the consequence of great holiness, and we often refer to the magi as the 'wise men'. So, in its origins, this type of image is associated with wisdom. Furthermore, liturgical texts from the twelfth century indicate that statues of this kind were actually used in dramatic performances representing the visitation of the magi.[2] At Epiphany – the feast of the Three Wise Men, on 6th January – it was the custom in some places to perform a play in which clerics who were dressed up as the three kings would go in search of the baby Jesus, and would find him and venerate him in the form of a statue of the Virgin in Majesty; and they would fall down and worship Christ before it. So when worshippers look upon an image of this kind, they are being enjoined to stand in the place occupied by the magi in Matthew's Gospel. It is now we who fall down and worship the child and offer him our gifts.

Let us consider, then, the symbolism encoded in these representations of the Seat of Wisdom. Christ has adult proportions, yet he is only a child in his mother's lap. He raises his hand in a gesture of authority, yet has the bare feet of a pauper. In the illuminations, he also has a cruciform halo behind his head. This collection of attributes is intended to tell us that the boy is God incarnate. The fact that he is a mature figure with his hand raised signifies his regal, or imperial, authority. The cruciform halo carries a similar indication of authority, since it is a symbol that was already used in representations of Christ as the Pantocrator, or Ruler of All. The book in Christ's left hand signifies that he is the Word of God, the second person of the Trinity. In the statue of Our Lady of Orcival (frontispiece), a magnificent Virgin in Majesty in the Diocese of Clermont, the book Christ holds in his left hand is marked with the Greek letters Alpha and Omega, the Beginning and the End, showing clearly the sacred and cosmic significance of the book's bearer. Yet, as it says in John's Gospel, 'the Word was made flesh and dwelt among us', meaning that Jesus is not only God eternal, but is also a human being who is present in time as one of us. And that is why he is only a small child on his mother's knee. The child's bare feet likewise signify his humanity. In symbolic commentaries on the Sciptures, the Church Fathers teach that references to Christ's head are references to Christ in his divinity, and references to his feet are references to his humanity. If you look back to the Renaissance paintings on Christmas cards, you will see that one of the three kings is often shown kissing the Lord's bare foot. This is because the event depicted here is the Epiphany, or Showing, that is, the showing of God in human form. The kings therefore venerate the humanity in which divinity is miraculously present. So the bare feet of the child in the Majesty statues point us to his real humanity. Thus, the God through whom all things were created has become one of his own creatures in Mary's womb.

Now the corollary of all this is, as we have seen in a previous chapter, that Mary, who is the mother of Christ, is simultaneously the Mother of God. This is the highest honour which could be bestowed upon any creature: other than being God incarnate, there is no superior condition which any human being could attain, because no-one could ever be more intimately united with the Godhead than this – to conceive and bear God in her very body. So, in the traditions of both the Catholic and Eastern Orthodox churches, the Virgin is said to be higher than the angels, and is crowned and enthroned as the Queen of Heaven.

It would be hard to overstate the extent of Mary's power and majesty in the culture of Western Europe in the eleventh and twelfth centuries. There has been no time in the history of Western Christianity when she has been accorded a higher status than she was during this period. For example, Eadmer of Canterbury, a pupil of St Anselm who is best known for having written the *Life of Anselm*, also wrote a work entitled *Tractate on the Conception of Saint Mary*,[3] a defence of the doctrine of Mary's Immaculate Conception. Working in the late eleventh century, the language in which Eadmer writes of the privileges that accrue to Mary in virtue of her being the Mother of God is almost entirely that of supreme authority. More than once he calls her 'mistress of the world and empress of the universe', and the reader is left in no doubt as to her cosmic dignity.

A very different example of Mary's being accorded extreme authority in the eleventh century is furnished by St Peter Damian (d. 1072), Bishop of Ravenna. He tells of a man who was visited in a dream by his deceased godfather, and, with the following words, was invited to follow him:

'Come see a spectacle that cannot fail to move you.' And he led him to the basilica of Saint Cecilia in the atrium of which he saw Saints Agnes, Agatha, and Cecilia herself in a choir of numerous resplendent holy virgins. They were preparing a magnificent throne which stood on a higher plane than those around it, and there the Holy Virgin Mary with Peter, Paul, and David, surrounded by a brilliant assemblage of martyrs and saints, came to take her place. While silence reigned in this holiest of gatherings and all respectfully remained standing, a woman who, though a pauper, wore a fur cloak, prostrated herself at the feet of the immaculate Virgin and implored her to have pity on the dead patrician, John. When she had repeated her prayer three times and received no answer, she added, 'You know, my lady, queen of the world, that I am that unfortunate woman who lay naked and trembling in the atrium of your great basilica [Santa Maria Maggiore]. That man [the patrician John] saw me and immediately took pity on me and covered me with the fur that I am wearing.' Whereupon Mary, blessed of God, said: 'The man for whom you are pleading was crushed by a great weight of crimes. But he had two good points: charity toward the poor and devotion, in all humility, to the holy places. In fact he often carried oil and kindling on his own shoulders for the lights of my Church.' The other saints testified that he did the same for their churches. The queen of the world ordered that the patrician be brought before the assembly. At once he was dragged in, bound and chained, by a horde of demons. Whereupon Our Lady ordered that he be delivered, and he went to swell the ranks of the saints [the elect]. But she ordered that the bonds from which he had just been set free be kept for another man, still living.[4]

Here, the Queen of Heaven has the power to save and to damn; she exercises that power to both ends, and she does so without direct reference to Christ.

What we see here is a certain symmetry between Christ and the Virgin. The second person of the Trinity, who has all things subject to him, descends to become a small creature in the Virgin's womb; and the Virgin, who is only a human woman, is elevated to share the power and authority of Christ himself. In an elegant movement of descent and ascent, the God who becomes human enables the woman who gave him his humanity to rise up and be enthroned on the seat which is next to the Deity.

Seat of Wisdom

In an image of the Seat of Wisdom, however, the Virgin is not only enthroned: she is herself a throne. For Christ is enthroned on her lap, and this is the primary meaning of the title 'Seat of Wisdom' as it is applied to the Virgin in Majesty. So let us turn now to think about the figure of Wisdom.

In the Hebrew Scriptures, Wisdom as a personal figure – as distinct from wisdom as a human attribute – should probably be understood in the first instance as an attribute of God. Wisdom directs men and women to lead good lives, and thus is associated with specifically moral action. But the workings of Wisdom are also perceived in the natural order of the non-human world: animals know how to build themselves homes, when the mating season is, and so on. The seasons likewise come in an ordered cycle. If human beings attend to the teachings of Wisdom, then our lives will be similarly properly ordered, in accordance with God's intention. Wisdom, then, governs the natural and the moral orders, and Wisdom is often personified as a female figure.

Some books of the Bible are known as 'Wisdom writings', for example, the Hebrew books of Proverbs, Ecclesiastes, and the Song of Songs, and the Greek books of the Wisdom of Solomon, Ecclesiasticus and Baruch. Much of this literature is attributed to King Solomon. Just as the first five books of the Bible, the Torah, are attributed to Moses, the great teacher and law-giver, and the Psalms are attributed to King David, the musician, so the biblical literature that is concerned with right living and with the discernment of Wisdom is attributed to King Solomon, reputedly the wisest of all men and women. One text that is particularly important when considering the Catholic cult of the Virgin Mary is Proverbs 8.22–31. In this numinous speech, Wisdom herself declares, 'The Lord created me at the beginning of his works, the first of his acts of old.' She then goes on to say that she was present before anything else was created – the earth, the sea, and so on. She says she was present with God, delighting in his works.

In the New Testament, Christian authors apply Old Testament texts about Wisdom to Christ. In I Corinthians, St Paul refers to Christ as 'the Wisdom of God' (1.24), and sees the world as existing through him (8.6). In John 1.1–5, the Word, who is Christ, is described in language that draws heavily upon Wisdom imagery. Christians have always continued to see Christ as Wisdom incarnate, yet, as we shall see, it was not only Christ, but other figures also, who came to be seen as endowed with the attributes of Holy Wisdom.

For the moment, however, let us ask: why is it that the figure of Wisdom should be enthroned, as Christ is seated upon his mother's lap in the Majesty statues? What is the significance of Wisdom's enthronement? Well, part of the reason is that Mary is the place in whom Christ resides, and for that reason she is often given titles such as 'altar', or 'throne of Grace'. But there is a more particular symbolism involved here. I have already mentioned that Solomon is seen in Scripture and tradition as one who is uniquely wise amongst men and women; and the books of II Kings and II Chronicles make much of Solomon's splendid throne:

> The king also made a great ivory throne, and overlaid it with pure gold. The throne had six steps and a footstool of gold, which were attached to the throne, and on each side of the seat were arm rests and two lions standing beside the arm rests, while twelve lions stood there, one on each end of the steps on the six steps. The like of it was never made in any kingdom. (II Chronicles 9.17–19)

Look again at the Eynsham manuscript illumination (Figure 4). Here are the Virgin and Child enthroned, and the Virgin is seated on a lion throne – intending you to call to mind King Solomon, and therefore Wisdom. To Christian authors of the twelfth century, the Old Testament was full of 'types' of characters from the Gospels. The word 'type' is derived from the Greek word *tupos*, meaning a blow, or strike. In English, the word is used in relation to printing, where we have the words 'typeface' and 'typewriter', since these make an imprint by striking a blow. A biblical *type*, therefore, is a person or action that bears a likeness, or imprint, of some other person or action. In particular, the men and women of the Old Testament were (and sometimes still are) seen to foreshadow the greater figures of the New – and especially Christ and the Virgin. So, for example, Abraham's sacrifice of Isaac is a type of the Father's sacrifice of the Son on the cross. Likewise, Solomon, the wise ruler, is a type of Christ, and the splendid throne on which he sits is a type of the Virgin, in whose body Christ resided.

The spiritual writer Adam of St Victor (d. 1180) wrote a hymn to the Virgin in which he says: 'You are the throne of Solomon ... white ivory foretells your chastity, red gold foretells your charity.'[5] So every detail of the throne becomes a type of some quality of the Blessed Virgin.

Sometimes the Queen of Sheba is seen as a type of the magi. She was a ruler noted for her wisdom and learning, who came to visit King Solomon. She asked him many questions, and, finding he could answer them all, had to acknowledge his superior wisdom. As the Queen of Sheba came to do homage to Solomon on his throne, so the magi are similarly wise rulers who come to do homage to Christ in the lap of the Virgin.

A sermon attributed to Peter Damian identifies Mary with Solomon's throne, and continues:

Our Solomon [Christ], [who is] not only wise but [is] indeed the Wisdom of the Father, ... has prepared a throne, manifestly the womb of the chaste Virgin, in which sat that Majesty which shakes the world with a nod.[6]

This sermon says that the ivory of Solomon's throne is an image of Mary's virginity; and it then describes the gold with which the throne was covered, concluding: 'In like manner, God clothed the Virgin and was clothed in the Virgin.' Some of the Majesty statues are indeed gilded. The statue of Our Lady of Orcival (frontispiece), for example, is clothed in silver gilt. It is a carved wooden figure, covered in pieces of gilded silver, and seated upon a throne which is also covered in silver gilt. The Virgin is herself Solomon's throne; she is covered in the gold of majesty and honour which God has bestowed upon her, as he himself was covered by the womb which she bestowed upon him.

Maria Sapientia

So far, we have seen several examples of a certain symmetry between Our Lord and Our Lady. He takes her human condition, and she shares his heavenly one. She gives him the throne of her body, and he gives her the throne of judgement. She clothes him with flesh, and he clothes her with honour. But the most important symmetry that I am going to refer to here is still another one: namely, that as Christ is the Wisdom of God through whom the world is created, so Mary is the Wisdom of God through whom the world is renewed.

As we have seen, in the statues which are called 'Seat of Wisdom', it is not only Christ who is seated, or enthroned, but also Mary, and by the early Middle Ages, biblical texts concerning Holy Wisdom were used to refer to Mary herself. Ildefonsus of Toledo (617–67), a bishop and theologian who wrote a major work on Mary, uses words borrowed from the book of Ecclesiasticus (24.20–1), where they refer to Wisdom, in a hymn addressed to the Virgin:

The person who savours you, ardently desires you still,
still thirsts for your holy sweetness,
and always unfulfilled, confines his longing
to loving you and praising you.[7]

An identification between Mary and Wisdom became common in the high Middle Ages, due to the use of Wisdom texts in Marian liturgies – a usage which seems to date back to Alcuin of York (d. 804), who was official liturgist at the court of the Emperor Charlemagne, and whose work was influential in much subsequent Western liturgy. By Alcuin's time, it was not uncommon for texts concerning Holy Wisdom to be used in the liturgies for the feast days of virgins. Alcuin himself probably used a Wisdom text in the Mass for the feast of St Agatha, the virgin martyr. And in this instance, the reference being made is principally to the Wise Virgins of the Gospel: the virgin saint is the one who has chosen the path of wisdom and kept her lamp ready to welcome the bridegroom.[8] However, Alcuin uses Wisdom texts in several more contexts than this. He wrote a complete set of prayers for a Mass in honour of Holy Wisdom, and in these prayers Wisdom seems to be attributed with characteristics of both the second and third persons of the Blessed Trinity. Elsewhere, in a non-liturgical text, Alcuin identifies Wisdom explicitly with each of the three persons of the Trinity.[9] It is therefore most interesting that he wrote two votive masses of the Blessed Virgin – which were used on Saturdays, since Saturday is the day set aside for special veneration of Mary – and that in one of these Masses Alcuin includes the text beginning at Ecclesiasticus 24.9: 'From eternity, in the beginning, he created me, and for all the ages I shall not cease to be,' referring to Wisdom dwelling with the Lord. It seems clear that the use of these verses is intended in some way to designate Mary. Certainly, that is how it came to be understood within a very short space of time.

A Vatican manuscript of the tenth century includes a Mass for Our Lady's Birthday in which one of the lections is Proverbs 8.22 following 'The Lord possessed me at the beginning of his ways ...', and so on. The Gospel which is given for the same Mass is Christ's genealogy from the beginning of Matthew's Gospel. One modern commentator, Etienne Catta, describes this combination of readings as 'striking',[10] since it seems to suggest that the birth of the Virgin is analogous to Christmas, with Mary's creation from the beginning of time being rendered parallel to the Prologue to John's Gospel, whose opening words are, 'In the beginning was the Word', referring to Christ. As Christ was present from eternity, and in the fullness of time became flesh in his mother's womb, so Mary was in some manner present from the foundations of the world, and likewise was born when the time was right for her part in the fulfilment of God's plan. Proverbs 8.22–31 in fact came to be the standard reading at Mass for the feasts of Mary's Birthday (8th September) and of her Conception (8th December).

Now, is this association of Wisdom with Mary an example of imaginative hyperbole, or does it have some theological substance? When Wisdom readings were first applied to Mary, it was not claimed that they applied to her in the direct manner in which they applied, for example, to Christ – only that the language used in them could also be seen to be true in some sense of Mary as well. The Wisdom texts referred to Mary not literally, but by 'accommodation', or suitability. However, during later centuries, it came to be generally accepted that these texts could be taken to signify Mary directly. I am going to argue now that there is good reason underlying the instinct which led people to see an immediate connection between Mary and Holy Wisdom.

We have seen in a previous chapter the Christian doctrine which holds that the world is created *by* God the Father, *through* God the Son, *in the power of* the Holy Spirit. It is specifically as the one *through whom* the world is created that Christ is identified with Wisdom. We have also seen that, at Christ's conception, God the Son becomes himself the new creation through the agency of the Blessed Virgin Mary: she is not only the matter of which the new creation is formed, but also the moral agent by whom it takes life in the created world. So the original creation, God's first creation, is made through Christ, who is Wisdom, in eternity. But in the *new* creation, Christ is himself the work of creation. And this new creation in Christ is formed *through* his mother Mary. So it is now she who takes on the mantle of Holy Wisdom, *through whom* God does the work of creation. As the first creation was wrought *through* Holy Wisdom in the person of Christ, so the new creation, Jesus himself, is wrought *through* Holy Wisdom in the person of Mary. So in Mary, who is both the substance of the cosmos and a unique co-operator in the work of redemption, Wisdom is one with the material foundation of the universe. Not only is the relationship between Mary and her son cast in the image of that which exists between the first and second Persons of the Trinity, but it is also cast in the likeness of the relationship between the second Person of the Trinity and the order of creation.

By now it should be clear that the idea that in the Incarnation the world was restored, or created anew, through Mary, has a reputable history in Catholic Christianity. I quoted earlier from a sermon for Our Lady's birthday, in which she is compared to Solomon's throne. The same sermon says: 'Today she is born through whom we are all born again, whose honour the Almighty greatly desired, and in whom God established his throne.' St Anselm elaborates this theme considerably in one of his prayers to St Mary, comparing her in this instance to God the Father:

Heaven, stars, earth, waters, day and night, and whatever was in the
power or use of men was guilty;
they rejoice now, Lady, that they lost that glory, for a new and ineffable
grace has been given them through you.
...

O woman, uniquely to be wondered at, and to be wondered at for your
uniqueness,
by you the elements are renewed, hell is redeemed, demons are trampled
down and men are saved; even the fallen angels are restored to their place.
O woman full and overflowing with grace, plenty flows from you to
make all creatures green again.
O virgin blessed and ever blessed, whose blessing is upon all nature,
not only is the creature blessed by the Creator, but the Creator is
blessed by the creature too.
...

All nature is created by God and God is born of Mary. God created all
things, and Mary gave birth to God.
God who made all things made himself of Mary, and thus he
refashioned everything he had made.
He who was able to make all things out of nothing refused to remake
it by force, but first became the Son of Mary.
So God is the Father of all created things, and Mary is the mother of
all re-created things.
God is the Father of all that is established, and Mary is the mother of
all that is re-established.
For God gave birth to him by whom all things were made and Mary
brought forth him by whom all are saved.
God brought forth him without whom nothing is; Mary bore him without whom nothing is good.
O truly, 'the Lord is with you', to whom the Lord gave himself, that all
nature in you might be in him.[11]

So 'all nature' is *in* Mary, and is saved *through* her. It is for precisely this
reason that she may be called Wisdom.

We have seen now that Mary is in a certain sense identified with
Wisdom, and that there is an association between wisdom and the imagery
of sovereignty. The three kings, for example, are wise men. The Queen
of Sheba and King Solomon are wise rulers. Christ as Wisdom, and Mary

as the Seat of Wisdom, are depicted as regal figures. And perhaps this is not surprising, since no virtue is to be sought in a governor if not that of wisdom. As it is by Wisdom that God orders the creation, so it is only by wisdom that human beings can rightly govern their own affairs, both in relation to other human beings and in relation to other creatures. Furthermore, this is true not only for those endowed with official authority, but for all men and women who are of an age and mental capacity at which they can take any responsibility for their own lives. All are called to act wisely in their relationships with other people, and in their treatment of the animals, plants and minerals with which we are in constant contact.

There are traditions concerning kingship within the island of Britain which may be read as parables concerning the wise government of the land, and I turn now to these traditions in order to see further how, embedded within traditions of Marian devotion, there is an awareness of the sanctity of the physical creation and of humanity's responsibility to treat it with reverence.

Our Lady's Dowry

In 1399, the year of the death of Richard II, the Archbishop of Canterbury, Thomas Arundel, wrote the following words:

> The contemplation of the great mystery of the Incarnation has drawn all Christian nations to venerate her from whom come the first beginnings of our redemption. But we English, being the servants of her special inheritance and her own Dowry, as we are commonly called, ought to surpass others in the fervour of our praises and devotions.[12]

From this it seems clear that 'Our Lady's Dowry' was in use as a title for England in the late Middle Ages, and after the Reformation it became very popular amongst English Roman Catholics, who have continued to use it down to the present day. Yet what does this title mean? And what is its origin?

A dowry is the possession that a bride takes into her marriage. But although Mary had a human husband, Joseph, the reference to her dowry certainly does not relate to this marriage: the Western church had no marked devotion to St Joseph until the fifteenth century,[13] and Mary had had bridal language and imagery applied to her for many centuries before this time. The earliest reference to Mary as a bride may be from the great fourth-century poet, Ephraem of Syria. In a flurry of symbols of kinship and affinity, Ephraem says that Christ gave birth to Mary (since she is reborn as all Christians are in baptism), that she is also his sister (since both Mary and Christ are descendents of their father David), that she is his mother (since she bore him in her womb), and also his bride, because Christ is chaste.[14] By the beginning of the Middle Ages, the doctrine that Mary was perpetually a virgin was in effect the Church's official teaching, but even from earliest centuries, the poetic image of Mary as a bride indicated that she was engaging in a symbolically marital union with a spouse who was supernatural, not human.

To understand this, it is helpful to refer to the teaching from St Paul's letter to the Christians at Ephesus (Ephesians 5.21–33). He quotes words from the story of Adam and Eve in the book of Genesis: '"a man shall leave his father and mother and be joined to his wife, and the two shall become one flesh."' And he continues: 'This mystery is a profound one, and I am saying that it refers to Christ and the Church' (vv.31–2). Addressing the church at Corinth, Paul says, 'I feel a divine jealousy for you, for I betrothed you to Christ to present you as a virgin bride to her one husband. But I am afraid that as the serpent deceived Eve by his cunning, your thoughts will be led away from a sincere and pure devotion to Christ' (2 Corinthians 11.2–3). The Church is the community of Christians to whom Christ's mission is entrusted now that Christ is no longer present on earth as a man. As well as being a social and political institution, the Church has a mystical character, and one aspect of that mystical character is its unique union with the Lord, Jesus Christ. This union is often expressed in terms of the union between husband and wife. Now, the Virgin Mary is very closely associated with the Church, not least insofar as she is the Church's 'type', or image, so that those things which are said about Mary – such as that she is a virgin or a mother – are symbolically true of the Church as well. And this symbolism can work in reverse: as the Church is the bride of Christ, Mary also may be seen as a bride. She is the 'virgin bride' who is not led away from 'pure devotion to Christ'. Indeed, her overshadowing by the Holy Spirit and her giving birth to God incarnate mean that she does have a uniquely close union with the Lord. So Mary's nuptial celebration, in some mysterious way, is with God himself, and it is to this divine marriage that she takes her dowry.

How England acquired the title 'Our Lady's Dowry' is not truly known. In the seventeenth century, some writers said that it derived from the

English people's great devotion to the Virgin. A painted panel, in the possession of English people in Rome in the early part of the seventeenth century, depicted a king presenting 'the globe or patterne of England' to the Blessed Virgin, saying, 'This is your dowry, Holy Virgin; therefore rule it, Mary.'[15] It is not certain who the king was, but the most common interpretation is that it was Richard II (1367–1400), and that he may have formally consecrated England to be 'Our Lady's Dowry'.

The story which holds that Richard made such a consecration runs as follows. In Westminster Abbey, the seat of sacred authority in England, where Richard was himself crowned king, there used to be a shrine of the Virgin Mary at which she was invoked by the now obscure title, 'Our Lady of Pew'. In 1381, at the time of the Peasants' Revolt, Richard went personally to confront Wat Tyler, the peasants' leader, in the hope of subduing his rebellious subjects; and before he set out for the encounter, which took place at Smithfield, Richard went to Westminster to pray at the shrine of St Edward the Confessor and also to Our Lady of Pew. He vowed that if the revolt were quelled, then he would dedicate England as the Virgin's dowry. In the event, Richard's endeavour was successful, and England thus became Our Lady's Dowry as an ex voto offering from a grateful king.[16]

This story, however, raises as many questions as it answers. For where would such a title have come from in the first place? Is it just the romantic whim of a young king who wanted to do something noble for his heavenly queen? Or was he appealing to a tradition that was already well established, and to a title that would have resonance with his fellow countrymen and women? I suggest the latter, and that traces of that tradition may be found elsewhere in medieval literature, and point us to a spiritual significance to this title which might still be fruitful today.

The spirit of the land

Although the government and jurisdiction of Britain has always been divided amongst different groups and rulers – between Scots and English, for example – it is probable that British people, whatever their ancestry or language, have normally had a sense of belonging to the island as such. As the spiritual author, Caitlín Matthews, writes: 'For every separate kingdom which forms the United Kingdom, there is an inner home into which its people yearn longingly to enter.'[17] There is a kind of cultural identity that comes from living in the place, an identity generated by features of the land itself, and constituted by traditions such as the legends of King

Arthur, who, it is said, will finally return from the dead to re-establish sacred rule in Britain. In the later Middle Ages, English monarchs often wanted to extend their control over Wales, and could use the ideology of the island's unity to try to legitimate their domination of the whole of southern Britain. Thus, for example, King Henry VII, of Welsh descent, named his eldest son Arthur, as though pointing to the day when the king desired by all Britons would rule again. Yet there are also medieval stories about Britain, written in Welsh, which are not so obviously concerned with political domination, and which perhaps embody part of the tradition to which the English kings were appealing, since they retain a memory – or vision – of a more united island. Some of these stories are contained in the *Mabinogion*; they portray the island of Britain as sacred, and suggest the mythical background to the title 'Our Lady's Dowry'.

One such story is *The Dream of Macsen Wledig*, or 'Macsen the Ruler'.[18] According to the legend, Macsen was the Roman Emperor. One day he went out hunting with his vassals, and after they had rested for lunch, he fell asleep and had a dream. In his dream, he was transported over mountains and plains, and eventually across sea, until he came to the fairest island in the world. He then crossed the island, until he came again to sea, with mountains and a plain extending to the mouth of a river, where there was a castle on a coastline facing an island. On entering the castle, Macsen found two lads and an old man, together with a maiden whose beauty was as dazzling as the sun, so that it was impossible to look upon her. She wore white silk with gold clasps, and a surcoat and mantle of gold brocade. They embraced one another and sat together in her golden chair. Then Macsen awoke from his sleep, and was so in love with the maiden that he could think of nothing but trying to find her in order to seek her hand in marriage.

After a year of fruitless searching, Macsen sent out thirteen messengers to follow exactly the journey on which he had been taken in his dream. Everything turned out to be as he had seen it in his sleep, but now they discovered the identities of the places they were visiting. Across the sea, the beautiful island was Britain, the mountains were Eryri (Snowdonia) from where they could see Môn (Anglesey), and the castle was at Aber Seint (Caernarvon). And inside the castle, they found the fair maid, Elen. Macsen's marriage suit was successful, and he came to Britain to marry Elen, who was a virgin and thus could command a maiden fee from her new husband. The fee she named included 'for her father the Island of Britain from the North Sea to the Irish Sea, and the three adjacent islands, to be held under the Empress of Rome'.[19]

Seven years later, Macsen was deposed as Emperor of Rome, so he returned to reclaim his dominion, and while Elen looked on, her brothers and a small group of Britons recaptured the city for her sake.

This story has generated much scholarly debate – for example, concerning which historical emperor underlies the character of Macsen. He seems to be a composite figure, made up of historical and legendary characters, his name deriving from Magnus Maximus (r. 383–88).[20] The figure of Elen has likewise been the subject of such discussion, and it seems likely that there are strong connections between Elen and St Helen, who, by tradition, was the British mother of the emperor Constantine, and who went on pilgrimage to the Holy Land, where she found the relic of the 'true cross' on which Christ had been crucified.[21] One theory, however, suggests that, whatever else she may signify, Elen of the Hosts (as she is titled) is a personification of the sovereignty of the island of Britain, whom the emperor must marry if he is to gain authority in the land. Thus, it is only because of Elen's acceptance that the emperor gains the right to govern. Matthews writes, 'the monarch holds the land by right of his union with her, by his championship of her freedoms and privileges which he lawfully assumes'.[22] The king of Britain acquires his throne by being symbolically married to the island, in the person of Elen, and he then has a sacred duty to defend and promote the welfare of both the land and its people. This theory of Elen's identity treats the story as the remnant of a pagan myth which may once have been tied to some ritual wedding between the king and the land; but even without such an earlier myth or ritual, it provides a coherent interpretation of the story as it stands.

The Wilton Diptych

If we allow that the theory that Elen is the sovereignty of the island may be correct, then it is perhaps not too extravagant to suggest that a notion of just this kind underlies the Christian tradition that England is Our Lady's Dowry. The land is not now the habitation or incarnation of Elen, but the treasured possession of the Virgin Mary, and the king is not himself married to the land, but makes the country the Virgin's gift to a divine marriage, thereby rendering himself, as England's ruler, the custodian of a holy, and even heavenly, realm. This suggestion is reinforced by a consideration of a well-known painting which represents both Richard II and the Blessed Virgin Mary: namely, the double panel known as the Wilton Diptych (Figure 5), housed in the National Gallery in London.

Figure 5. The Wilton Diptych, National Gallery, London

The painting shows Richard II kneeling before the Virgin and Child, and may have been commissioned by the king himself. The image is modelled on representations of the Adoration of the Magi, or the visit of the three kings. Behind Richard there are two other kings of England, both of them canonized saints: St Edmund the Martyr (841–69), the East Anglian king who was killed by the Danes, and St Edward the Confessor (1003–66). At his coronation, Richard wore items of clothing that were reputed to have belonged to each of these saints. The third figure presenting Richard to the Virgin is St John the Baptist, a cousin of the Lord and the most important saint after his mother Mary. Richard's birthday was 6 January, which is the feast of the Epiphany, when the Church celebrates the coming of the magi.

These four figures are situated in the left-hand panel, on barren ground which represents earth. On the right, the Virgin and Child with angels are congregated on a carpet of flowers, and are evidently in Heaven. One of the angels holds a banner bearing the cross which signifies the Resurrection, but which is also the cross of St George, the patron saint of England. The angels all wear a brooch in the form of a hart, which was Richard's own emblem. Symbols of England are thus present in the heavenly realm. The mantle which Richard is wearing resembles those which he wore to receive his second wife, Isabelle of France, in 1396, and those worn by a procession of ladies and armed men on the occasion of Isabelle's coronation.[23] The robe thus bears an association with both marriage and accession to a throne.

It is possible that the Wilton Diptych is another representation of Richard dedicating England to be Our Lady's Dowry. If so, then the painting's strong association of earthly kings with the heavenly state may evoke the paradisical qualities of Elen's land as described in *The Dream of Macsen*.

It is interesting to observe that the description of Elen – with her brilliant gold and her beauty that is sunlike in its dazzling splendour – suggests solar attributes, as if she has some particular personal connection with the sun. In Christian tradition, both the Church and the Virgin Mary were, from early centuries, identified with the Woman of the Apocalypse, who appears in the biblical book of the Apocalypse (or Revelation). This woman is described as 'clothed with the sun, with the moon beneath her feet, and on her head a crown of twelve stars' (Apocalypse 12.1), and she appears at the inauguration of God's heavenly kingdom on earth. Medieval manuscripts show Mary as the woman clothed with the sun, and anyone familiar with this tradition is likely to be reminded of it in reading the description of Elen.

One obvious difference between the story of Macsen and the tradition concerning Our Lady's Dowry is that, whereas the *Mabinogion* story is concerned with the island of Britain, the later tradition is concerned only with England. Yet by looking more closely at the Wilton Diptych, and again making a comparison with stories from the *Mabinogion* collection, we can see that one only has to scratch the surface of words which name the political entity of England to find beneath them the natural formation of the island of Britain.

The White Tower

In the story of *Branwen Daughter of Llyr*,[24] Bendigeidfran is crowned king of Britain, 'the island of the mighty', in London. To form an alliance between the two countries, Bendigeidfran's sister Branwen marries the King of Ireland. This marriage leads, by a complicated route, to war between the British and the Irish, which culminates in the men of Britain being defeated in battle in Ireland. Branwen is said to be one of the Three Matriarchs of Britain, and Bendigeidfran, who has been the Britons' main hope of success in battle, is a giant, a figure of supernatural proportions and powers. Branwen's name means 'white crow' or 'white raven', and that of her brother also means 'blessed crow' or 'blessed raven'. After the defeat by the Irish – more truly described as a slaughter in which neither side has the victory – only seven British men escape, and on Bendigeidfran's own orders, they cut off his head and take it back to Britain, accompanied also by Branwen. The head continues speaking, and remains the living presence of Bendigeidfran amongst them. Eventually, again in fulfilment of the King's instructions, they take the head to London, where they bury it in the White Mount; and 'no plague would ever come across the sea to this Island so long as the head was in that concealment'.[25]

We are not told the location of the White Mount, but the city of London is built on a gravel mound which includes the elevation on which the Tower of London is constructed. Everyone who has visited the Tower knows that there are ravens living there, and that for as long as they remain there, Britain will be protected from invasion. Ravens, evidently, are sacred to Bendigeidfran – or perhaps are even his incarnation – and many commentators believe that the White Mount is the place where the White Tower, which is the oldest part of the Tower of London, was built.[26] The White Tower was built in the eleventh century; but at the turn of the third century, the Romans had enclosed the White Tower mound within the walls of the city of London, and, curiously, at this point the Roman wall made a detour: a building stood in the way, on the site where the chapel of the White Tower now stands, and instead of knocking the building down (as was done elsewhere) so that the wall could continue in a straight line, the Romans skirted around the older building and left it standing within the city wall. We have no way of knowing what was the use or significance of this building, but evidently, the Tower mound already housed a place of importance by the end of the second century.[27]

By the time of the reign of Richard II, the Tower of London had become associated in the minds of the English with the sovereignty of England, rather than the island of Britain, and the Virgin's protection was considered to fall especially upon English monarchs. A medieval legend held that the oil for the anointing of the kings of England had been given by the Blessed Virgin herself to St Thomas Becket, the martyred Archbishop of Canterbury, together with a prophecy that the fifth subsequent king of England would re-conquer the Holy Land. It was said that the oil was lost (a rather extraordinary act of carelessness!), and that the phial containing it was re-discovered in the Tower in 1399.[28]

If we turn back to the Wilton Diptych, we find that it contains a hidden image which seems to indicate the folklore of the Tower. When the painting was cleaned in 1991, it was found that the orb of the banner contained a tiny painting, only half an inch in diameter (Figure 6). This mysteriously small image shows a green island with a white castle or tower upon it, and a ship sailing towards it across sea that was originally silvered. Now, although the seventeenth-century accounts of the painting in Rome report that it depicted the king holding 'the globe or patterne of England', the orb of the Wilton Diptych shows an island, which therefore cannot be only England, but which might signify Britain as a whole. In Shakespeare's play *Richard II* (Act II, Scene 1), John of Gaunt speaks of England as 'this precious stone set in the silver sea', an expression which almost seems to be a description of the miniature in the Diptych. And even if the speech expresses sixteenth-century English ambitions to conquer the whole of Britain, it surely depends for its effect upon the summoning up of an already existing sense of the island's integrity – a sense which, I suggest, underlies all the mythology that I have been considering here.

In the light of the traditions concerning the Tower of London, and – if the foregoing speculation is accurate – the White Tower in particular, the presence of a white tower in the Diptych seems to offer further circumstantial evidence in support of the idea that this painting is intended to evoke associations with a tradition about the sanctity of the island. John of Gaunt also refers to his native land as 'this other Eden, demi-paradise ... this blessed plot', and thereby calls to mind heavenly qualities of the island such as those described in *The Dream of Macsen Wledig*, or suggested by the incorporation of English emblems in Heaven in the Wilton Diptych. It is as though these texts and images contain allusions to a whole world of popular mythology which has been lost, but some of whose elements, I shall suggest, we may do well to recover.

Sacred duty

In the mythology of the king's marriage to the country, a central element is the responsibility of the ruler to defend and promote the welfare of the land and its people. As in the notion of kingship as it is applied to Israel in the Old Testament, the ruler is not entitled to act on his own whim or for his own convenience: he has a sacred duty to husband the land in the inter-

Figure 6. The orb from the Wilton Diptych

ests of its welfare, to enable it to flourish. This means that if the land or its inhabitants suffer – for example, from famine, drought or military defeat – then it is likely to be the king who will be held to account for the misfortune because of his implied misrule. Conversely, a king who is seen to be a bad ruler will fall under divine censure.

The historian Sheridan Gilley sees an obligation of this kind to be implied in Richard II's consecration of England as Our Lady's Dowry, and in the corresponding iconography of the Wilton Diptych.[29] In medieval political theory, a distinction was drawn between the king's *office* and his *person*. His office was a sacred one, incurring sacred duties, and whilst those actions which counted as 'personal' would have no bearing on his performance of his office, unworthy actions which were deemed to relate to his official status could constitute a violation of sacred trust and effectively disinherit the monarch. Richard II was an unpopular ruler who was eventually deposed because, according to his accusers, he had violated his coronation oath by acting 'in great prejudice of the people and in dishersion of the crown of England'. In the Wilton Diptych, we see Richard kneeling before the Queen of Heaven, making 'that most binding of all forms of social cement, the vow, in which overlord and vassal exchange promises, promises as binding on the one as on the other'. But Richard 'forgot the meaning of his symbols', and so the diptych implies 'that Richard was forsworn, that he had simply not kept his part of the promise'.[30] Unlike Macsen, the emperor who makes Britain flourish and thus is faithful to Elen, by whose authority he rules, Richard does not honour his commitment to England and the Blessed Virgin, and in his misrule, Mary's authority does not hold sway. Richard was eventually imprisoned and murdered.

Macsen is a character from British mythology, and Richard II from English history, yet each can serve as a representative figure for a different way of living in the land on which God has placed us. That land is a heavenly treasure, and in much Catholic writing, Mary is seen as the treasurer of God's graces. Since she is the mother of Christ himself, she is the bearer and carer of God's highest blessing, and may thus be seen as entrusted with the protection and distribution of every precious gift that God bestows. The earth, air, heat and water which sustain us are among the first and greatest of God's gifts, and all men and women, in greater or smaller measure, hold the sacred trust of a regent in ensuring their welfare. We may be like Macsen in respecting our land, or like Richard in disregarding it. We may honour the sacred flame of Our Lady of the Taper, or we may act with dishonour and extinguish it for ever. If England and this island is Our Lady's Dowry, then it is the Mother of God who is honoured when we care for it, or scorned when we abuse it; and if we disinherit ourselves by creating a wasteland in place of Paradise, then it will be God who will finally call us to account for our actions, when we have completed our pursuit of a destiny far worse than that imposed upon Richard II by his fellow countrymen.

Honouring the wild

The choice between wisdom and folly, then, is the choice between reverence for a Godbearing creation and contempt for creation's God. So failure to acknowledge the presence of God in any aspect of our lives almost always has destructive consequences.

Since 1991, a dispute has been underway concerning the future of Roineabhal, a mountain on the Hebridean island of Harris. A roadstone company sought permission to quarry there, and a public enquiry was held in 1994–95 to consider the arguments for and against the application. In 1999, the Inquiry recommended that permission to quarry be granted; but that recommendation was not accepted by the body with the relevant powers, the Scottish Executive, who refused to grant permission, on the grounds that they had a duty to protect an officially designated National Scenic Area. Since then, the roadstone company concerned has been pursuing an appeal against this decision.

At the Inquiry, the arguments in favour of the quarry included economic benefits to the local community and to Scotland as a whole. The arguments against included damage to wildlife, the inconvenience of noise to local inhabitants, potential damage to the local fishing industry, and threats to local culture, including the Gaelic language. It was also argued that Sunday Sabbath observance would be threatened by seven-day working, and opposition was expressed to the consequences that quarrying would have for the nearby church of St Clement's: 'The effects of noise, vibration and air overpressure, together with the view into the quarry workings, would be to the detriment of [the] peace and sanctity of the churchyard.'[31] These concerns for Sabbath observance and the sanctity of the churchyard have an ostensibly religious character to them, but in fact they are based on a concern to respect the customs and environment of the local human community, not on religious values as such.

However, the Inquiry did also hear evidence from three witnesses who argued for the sacred character of the land itself. Among these was the

Presbyterian theologian Donald McLeod, who contended that '[t]heologically, the primary function of the creation is to serve as a revelation of God', which means that humanity has a responsibility to protect nature.[32] The arguments concerning the sanctity of the land were skated over in the Inquiry's final report, apparently being considered subordinate to economic and cultural considerations. But Kay Milton, an anthropologist commenting upon the Inquiry's findings, observes that, 'even if the decision makers had thought [the sacredness of the land] the most important issue, they could not have said so, because such views have no legitimacy in an arena constrained by the conventions of economic and scientific rationality.'[33] Yet a good case could be made for saying that arguments for nature conservation are almost always undergirded by a sense of the sanctity of the natural world, and that arguments on other grounds, such as scientific importance or recreational value, are secondary to that primary motivation.

The discussion of nature conservation, such as that described above, raises the question of what we mean by the word 'nature' at all. Is it indeed something that is implicitly 'sacred'? There are many different senses in which the term 'nature' is employed in everyday language, and several of these are implied – or even explicitly evoked – in Christian doctrine and devotion relating to the Virgin Mary.

Let us start with reference to one connotation that the word *nature* frequently carries, namely, that of *wilderness*, or the state of being free of human influence. It is in this sense that scientists sometimes speak of what happens 'in nature', as distinct from what happens 'in the laboratory', conditions in the laboratory being controlled by human investigators. Visitors to wildlife sites say that the presence of animals acting without the human constraint imposed by a farm, a zoo or a household generates a sense of being 'close to nature'. And areas of uncultivated forest or other wilderness are commonly described as being in their 'natural' state. Nature in this sense may be judged favourably or unfavourably: the wilderness may be desired or feared, but either way, it has almost always been perceived as enormously powerful – indeed, as possessing a power comparable to that of the sacred objects and supernatural beings which men and women venerate, celebrate or placate in religious ritual.

The hymn popularly ascribed to St Patrick and commonly known as 'St Patrick's Breastplate' begins with the words, 'I bind unto myself today / The strong name of the Trinity', and continues by invoking the mysteries of Christ's life and the powers of the angels and saints, before arriving at an invocation of natural, as well as supernatural, beings:

I bind unto myself today
The virtues of the starlit heaven,
The glorious sun's life-giving ray,
The whiteness of the moon at even,
The flashing of the lightning free,
The whirling wind's tempestuous shocks,
The stable earth, the deep salt sea,
Around the old eternal rocks.[34]

For the physical heaven and earth participate in and show forth the splendour of the celestial home of God.

In Christian tradition, the most sacred being who is not also divine is Mary the Mother of God, and she bears many attributes of sacred power which may also be associated with untamed nature. For example, she is both a virgin and a mother – a state which some authors have compared to the virgin forest, being both outside man's control and at the same time abundantly fruitful.[35] In an essay on the symbolic meanings of the Virgin Mary in Christianity, the psychotherapist Roger Horrocks writes: 'Our modern sense of ecology has begun to teach us again that the virgin must be preserved – for example, the virgin rain-forest. Its virginity is a fountain of life, and human penetration has often come to despoil and wreck it.'[36]

Equally, one might point to the doctrine that Mary is *immaculate* (literally, 'without stain'), or sinless. In Christian understanding, as mentioned above, human sin is what has tarnished and spoilt a world that God created as wholly good; so Mary's freedom from sin can signify both nature and humanity restored to, and surpassing, that original purity: human and non-human nature transfigured into a vigorous state of health, which begins to be possible only in a world that is purged of every kind of pollution.

However, this notion of nature as that which is untouched, unstained by human intervention, is not the only concept we have of nature, and it is not always the most helpful one. For when seen from another perspective, we are ourselves natural beings, composed of the same elements as the world we inhabit, and able to recognize a kinship with animal, vegetable, mineral and other creatures. Thus, St Francis of Assisi's famous Canticle of the Creatures calls upon Brother Sun and Sister Moon, Mother Earth and Brother Death, to praise their creator. Moreover, men and women have to co-operate continuously with natural forces for survival, and the relationship between humanity and the natural world may be either destructive or fruitful. Horticulture and agriculture may drain the goodness out of the earth and kill it, or they may enrich the soil, fostering new life. In the world of dense human habitation and technological sophistication which we have created, many varieties of wildlife and other aspects of the natural world are at the mercy of men and women, and it is human agency that determines whether or not they survive. So there are certain respects in which humanity and nature cannot be separated from one another.

Here also the Virgin Mary is an emblematic figure. When Adam and Eve eat the fruit of the tree of the knowledge of good and evil, they introduce evil into the world. And according to the story in Genesis 2–3, the curse that follows upon their actions affects not only their relationship with God and with one another, but also their relationship with the whole material world, and especially the earth from which they were made. Because of Adam, the ground is cursed (Genesis 3.17), and he will have to toil with the sweat of his brow to gain food (3.19), whilst Eve will suffer pain in what is otherwise the blessing of childbirth (3.16). Yet the Virgin Mary – in whom is restored what was lost in Eve – is without sin. This means that she is a human person whose will is perfectly conformed to the will of God and who enjoys right relationships with her fellow creatures.

Yet the word *nature* usually carries the connotation of a power that is clearly beyond, and greater than, that which can be exercised by humanity. That is to say, even allowing for the many ways in which men and women are inextricably bound to nature, there remains what the geographer Bill Adams calls 'its vital wildness'. However much men and women try to command or co-operate with 'nature', there may always be some unintended, and often unpredictable, consequences of human action. In this connection, we might think of global climate change caused by the chemical processes of modern industry. And even apart from human intervention, there are always surprises around the corner: no-one expects the onset of new diseases, such as AIDS. Adams comments: 'Nature on one level is constrained by human action, and lives in the spaces created by human economy, society and culture, but on another level its very naturalness consists in its capacity to survive and act *outside* human control.'[37] This transcendent character is one aspect of the natural world's sacredness. Indeed, perhaps all human sense of the sacred derives from a primary sense of our physical surroundings as both intimate and otherworldly, both precious and terrible. If so, then it is not surprising that a society which has lost a sense of the sacred is also a society which holds the natural world in scorn. Human beings have a choice: we may respect the forces of nature and hope to flourish, or we may treat them with contempt and most probably perish.

Why this should be the case is shown with particular force in the writing of John Scotus Erigena. John wrote a remarkable work entitled *On the Division of Nature*, in which he discusses the nature of the created world and its relationship to God. John begins by saying that Nature is the general term for all things that exist, and he sees nature as divided into four basic species, according to four differences. The differences are between that which is 'creating and not created', that which is 'created and creating', that which is 'created and not creating', and that which is 'neither creating nor created'. The first category, that which is *creating and not created*, refers to God, the source of all things. The second category, that which is *created and creating*, consists of what John calls the 'Primordial Causes'. These are 'creations' directly from God, including Wisdom, by which the world is made and sustained, and which subsist in Christ. The third category, that which is *created and not creating*, corresponds to what Christians would ordinarily call the creation, or the universe, both material and spiritual. The fourth category, that which is *neither creating nor created*, is God's own self as the end to which all things tend and in whom they have their fulfilment. The first and fourth of John's categories of Nature thus refer to God, the origin and end of the universe. So God is included within the general term 'Nature'.[38] John explains this surprising move by making it plain that the inclusion of God under the heading of Nature does not mean that God is included within creation. On the contrary, God is, as John's four differences spell out, uncreated. However, God is placed within the analytical category of Nature because

> ... he is the Beginning of all things and is inseparable from every universe that he has created and (is that) without which it cannot subsist. For in him are all things immutably and essentially; and he is the Division [the beginning] and Collection [the end] of the universal creature, and Genus and Species and Whole and Part although he is neither genus nor species nor whole nor part of anything, but all these are from him and in him and to him.[39]

This implies that if we consider any aspect of 'nature' without constantly taking account of its place in relation to the God who is its origin, its destiny and its entire sustenance, then we simply fail to understand nature's true character.

A similar idea is represented in the work of Ramon Llull, who may have

been influenced by Erigena. One of Llull's favourite images is that of the
ladder, or stairway. He sees the whole of existence as ordered in grades,
from the basic elements, upwards through orders of the material world
(such as rock and plants), to human beings, who are both material and
spiritual, and thence on up through the spiritual realms of heaven
and angels, culminating in God on the final rung. God is in fact present in
every lower order of being, and it is precisely this that is indicated by his
being included in the Ladder of Nature at all. For one might be tempted to
suggest that, since God is the Creator whilst everything else on the ladder
is created, God should not properly be included in this scheme – that the
Creator is radically different, and that the inclusion of God on one of the
steps undermines our awareness of this difference. Against this objection,
we must see that if we do not include God on the scale of nature, then we
are in danger of forgetting that it is in God that all things have their beginning and their end and that there is nowhere where God is not. Indeed, the
exclusion of God from humanity's consideration of the natural world may
be one of the very things that has led us to abuse and destroy it.

Nature's 'essential wildness', its transcendent power, derives quite precisely from its origin and subsistence in God, who is indeed beyond any
human power – who is entirely wild in the sense of being completely
uncontrollable by human agency.

Now, Mary the Godbearer is the Chaos that pervades all material
things, who subsists in God and in whom God is omnipresent. To set oneself
at war with nature is to fight against one's own being, its sacred origins in
God, and God dwelling within it. Llull understands 'sin' to consist of the
attempt to return ourselves or other beings to the nothing out of which we
are made,[40] that is, to try to go against the existence that comes from, and
subsists in, God. To maintain things in being and assist their flourishing is
to do good; to destroy things and to go against God's good creation is to do
evil. Fundamentally, there is being and there is nothing. Everything that
is in being is what John Scotus Erigena calls 'Nature', and is the work of
God's Goodness and Wisdom. Apart from this, there is privation, which is
the same as evil. So the sacred responsibility of humanity is to work always
with Wisdom for being, for goodness, for Nature. Mary is the bearer of that
Wisdom and is cast in Wisdom's own likeness. She is physically the mother
of God incarnate, and has been taken, body and soul, into the glory of heav-
en. In her, the destiny of all creatures to be bearers of God is already antic-
ipated, and God's desire to glorify them is already realized. In Mary we
glimpse both humanity and all nature in their final perfection.

Notes

1 Goullet, M., and Iogna-Prat, D., 'La Vierge en Majesté de Clermont-Ferrand', in Iogna-Prat, D. *et al.* (eds), *Marie: Le culte de la Vierge dans la société médiévale*, Beauchesne, Paris, 1996, 382–405.

2 Forsyth, I.H., *The Throne of Wisdom: Wood Sculptures of the Madonna in Romanesque France*, Princeton University Press, Princeton, New Jersey, 1972, 49–59.

3 Thurston, H. and Slater, P. (eds), *Eadmeri Monachi Cantuariensis Tractatus de Conceptione Sanctae Mariae*, Herder, Freiburg-im-Breisgau, 1904.

4 Quoted in Le Goff, J., *The Birth of Purgatory*, Scholar Press, Aldershot, 1984, 179.

5 The hymn is discussed in Forsyth, *op. cit.*, 26–9.

6 Forsyth, *op. cit.*, 25.

7 Quoted in Berselli, C., and Gharib, G. (eds), *In Praise of Mary: Hymns from the First Millennium of the Eastern and Western Churches* (trans. P. Jenkins), St Paul Publications, Slough, 1981, 72.

8 Catta, E., 'Sedes Sapientiae', in du Manoir, H. (ed.), *Maria: Etudes sur la Sainte Vierge* VI, Beauchesne, Paris, 1961, 689–866, at 694.

9 Meyers, R.A., 'The Wisdom of God and the Word of God: Alcuin's mass "of Wisdom"', in Dudley, M. (ed.), *Like a Two-edged Sword: The Word of God in Liturgy and History*, Canterbury Press, Norwich, 1995, 39–59.

10 Catta, *op. cit.*, 696.

11 'Prayer to St. Mary (3)', 118–201, in Ward, B. (trans. and ed.), *The Prayers and Meditations of Saint Anselm*, Penguin, Harmondsworth, 1973, 118–21.

12 Cited in Bridgett, T.E., *Our Lady's Dowry: How England Gained that Title*, Burns & Oates, London, 1891, 1.

13 Warner, M., *Alone of All Her Sex: The Myth and the Cult of the Virgin Mary*, Quartet Books, London, 1978, 188–90.

14 Cited in Graef, H., *Mary: A History of Doctrine and Devotion*, Sheed & Ward, London, 1985 [two vols in one], Vol. 1, 57–8.

15 Bridgett, *op. cit.*, v–vii; quotation from p.v, citing British Library ms. Harley 360, f. 98, 6.

16 Elvins, M., '"The Dowry of Mary": The origins of the title and the shrines of Our Lady at Westminster', in *Walsingham: A Centenary Celebration*, Guild of Our Lady of Ransom, London, 1998, 41–8.

17 Matthews, C., *Mabon and the Mysteries of Britain: An Exploration of the Mabinogion*, Arkana, London and New York, 1987, 9.

18 *The Mabinogion* (trans. G. and T. Jones), Dent, London and New York, [Everyman's Library], 79–88.

19 *The Mabinogion*, 85.

20 Harbus, A., *Helena of Britain in Medieval Legend*, D.S. Brewer, Cambridge, 2002, 55–61.

21 Harbus, *op. cit.*, 61–3 and *passim*.

22 Matthews, *op. cit.*, 7.

23 Gordon, D., *Making and Meaning in the Wilton Diptych*, National Gallery Publications, London, 1993, 51.

24 *The Mabinogion*, 25–40.

25 *The Mabinogion*, 40.

26 Ronald Hutton writes that the head was laid at Tower Hill: *The Pagan Religions of the Ancient British Isles: Their Nature and Legacy*, Blackwell, Oxford, 1993, 197.

27 Lapper, I., and Parnell, G., *The Tower of London: A 2000-year History*, Osprey Publishing (for the Royal Armouries), Wellingborough, 2000, 8.

28 Gordon, *op. cit.*, 60.

29 Gilley, S., 'The Wilton Diptych: Sacral monarchy and the Virgin's dowry', in *Walsingham: A Centenary Celebration*, Guild of Our Lady of Ransom, London, 1998, 49–65, at 57–61.

30 Gilley, *op. cit.*, 60–1.

31 Link Quarry Group, 'Reasons for refusal', 12. Included on the website of Friends of the Earth Scotland (June 2002), www.foe-scotland.org.uk/nation/superquarry. More recent information can be found in McIntosh, A., 'Superquarry saga rumbles on', *Ecos: A Review of Conservation* 24(2), 2003, 63–7.

32 Milton, K., *Loving Nature: Towards an Ecology of Emotion*, Routledge, London and New York, 2002, 143.

33 Milton, *op. cit.*, 144.

34 This is the most commonly used translation, by C.F. Alexander.

35 Layard, J., 'The incest taboo and the virgin archetype', *Eranos Jahrbuch*, Vol. XII, 1945, 290–1; Hall, N., *The Moon and the Virgin: Reflections on the Archetypal Feminine*, The Women's Press, London, 1980, 11.

36 Horrocks, R., 'The divine woman in Christianity', in Pirani, A. (ed.), *The Absent Mother: Restoring the Goddess to Judaism and Christianity*, Mandala, London, 1991, 100–35, at 110–11.

37 Adams, W.M., *Future Nature: A Vision for Conservation,* Earthscan Publications, London, 1997, 103.

38 Eriugena, I.S., *Periphyseon (De Divisione Naturae)* Vol. I, Sheldon-Williams, I.P. (ed.), Dublin Institute for Advanced Studies, Dublin, 1968, 36–9.

39 Eriugena, I.S., *Periphyseon (De Divisione Naturae)* Vol. III, Sheldon-Williams, I.P. (ed.), Dublin Institute for Advanced Studies, Dublin, 1981, 30–3.

40 Lulio, R., *Libro de la Concepcion Virginal* [Latin text with Spanish trans. by A. de Zepeda], Baltazar Vivien, Brussels, 1664, 28–33.

Figure 7. Diego Velázquez: *The Immaculate Conception*,
National Gallery, London

9
Immaculate Conception

Among the great works of European painting, one of the best loved is Diego Velázquez's *Immaculate Conception* (Figure 7), which hangs in the National Gallery in London. It is a painting that represents not only the beginning of the Virgin's life, but also, in some measure, the world's beginning and its end. And this, indeed, is the subject of Mary's Immaculate Conception.

The doctrine of Mary's immaculate conception is concerned with the Virgin's own conception in the womb of her mother, St Anne. Specifically, the doctrine holds that, in virtue of the redeeming merits of Jesus Christ, Mary was given a special grace which preserved her from the stain of original sin from the first instant of her conception. The Immaculate Conception was defined as an article of Catholic faith by Pope Pius IX in 1854, after many centuries of controversy, and is both one of the richest and one of the most mysterious teachings of the Catholic tradition.[1]

The doctrine of original sin is a teaching peculiar to the Western church. Its founder is often considered to be St Augustine of Hippo (354–430), since it was he who first gave it a full exposition and defence. Ever since Adam and Eve fell from grace, humanity has been subject to the condition of original sin and its consequences: most particularly, to death. What this means is that, from the moment of conception, simply in virtue of being descendants of Adam and Eve, men and women are in some way guilty and set in opposition to God. This is quite apart from the actual sins that they commit during the course of their earthly lives. The guilt of original sin, as of sin in general, is removed by the grace that is given in baptism, although God may choose to bestow this grace by some other means. For example, it has traditionally been taught that John the Baptist was 'sanctified' (i.e., purified of original sin) in the womb of his mother Elizabeth at the time of the Visitation, when 'the babe leaped in her womb and Elizabeth was filled with the Holy Spirit' (Luke 1.41). Some of the consequences of original sin remain, however, even after the guilt has been removed. Physical death is one such consequence, and a certain propensity to sin – called *concupiscence* – is another.

How it is that original sin is transmitted from one generation to the next has never been formally defined, and theologians have disagreed about this. Augustine himself believed that it was connected to the lust experienced during sexual intercourse – that the devil was in the flesh, so that the body of anyone conceived in this way would be formed out of contaminated seed, which in turn would infect the person's soul. On this understanding, it would be only a virginal conception, such as that of Jesus, that could preserve anyone from original sin. Mary, as we have seen from the legends in the *Protevangelium of James*, was believed to have been conceived in the usual manner, which, by Augustine's argument, ought to mean that she was conceived in sin. But Augustine was somewhat reluctant to follow through the implications of his own reasoning, and declined to attribute original sin to Mary directly, preferring merely to remain silent on the subject of her radical sinlessness. Augustine's more austere interpreters, however, have always refused to concede that any exception could have been made for the Blessed Virgin, and have denied that she was immaculately conceived.

John Duns Scotus held a different understanding of original sin to that of Augustine. Taking the view that sin affects only the will, which is a faculty of the soul, and not the body, he did not think original sin was transmitted in the seed or the flesh. Adam and Eve had lost the original state of righteousness, or justice, in which they were created, and their descendants, having souls similar to those of their forebears, would likewise develop in the soul faculties that would be orientated away from God. However, he argued, just as the guilt of original sin can be washed away in baptism, so God can remove original sin by some other means if he so chooses. For this reason, it was quite possible for God to have given Mary this special grace at the moment of her conception. Working with the belief that prevention is better than cure, he argued that for Mary to be conceived without original sin would have been a superior form of redemption than for her to be conceived in sin and then purified of it. And since she was to be the Mother of God, it would have been part of God's providence that she, of all people, should have received this exceptional privilege. She may also have been preserved from some of the consequences of original sin, in particular, from concupiscence.

A third view of the transmission of original sin is given by Rámon Llull, in his defence of the Immaculate Conception.[2] Llull's view of the matter has never received official approval from the Church, but in several respects it seems to be the most satisfactory one. Llull believes that, in many cases, an actor's intention is all-important in determining the outcome of an action. In the case of the conception of a child, he believes that if a couple sincerely desire to conceive a child who will know and love God, a child whose human condition they desire to be united to that of Jesus Christ, then the child conceived of that union will start its life in a condition morally superior to that of a child conceived out of less noble motives. Now, just as the builder who builds a palace for a king chooses only the finest materials and the best workmen, so God will have willed that the woman who was to be the mother of his Son should be the worthiest human being possible. Accordingly, Llull argues that, when Anne and Joachim conceived the child who was to be the Mother of the Son of God, they must have had the holiest of intentions. God would have given them the grace to enable this, and the purity of the parents' desire would then have ensured the moral purity of the child whom they conceived. Llull also thinks that the holiness of this act would have meant that Anne and Joachim enjoyed greater carnal pleasure than any other couple have ever enjoyed during sexual intercourse!

Llull's argument has the virtue of restoring a unity to the physical and the spiritual – a unity that is lost in the formulation of Duns Scotus. Parental motives, sexual pleasure, and the moral character of the child conceived are all tied to one another in a manner that implies the necessary integrity of the human person and of our relationships with one another. Llull's case also has the virtue of tying the doctrine of the Immaculate Conception to the wider question of humanity's capacity for holiness: it is because that capacity is already there that Anne and Joachim can respond to God's grace and conceive a sinless infant. But the doctrine of the Immaculate Conception in itself points to the abiding goodness that underlies humanity and all God's creation.

It is possible to present the Immaculate Conception as a teaching that emphasizes Mary's exceptional character and thus her difference and distance from other men and women. Yet with this, as with other Marian doctrines, Mary's uniqueness points precisely to something that is true of all humanity and of all creation. For although it is only Mary who is without trace of sin, the conception of the woman in whom the Word of God is to take flesh and thus redeem the world is a cause for rejoicing, and the fact that Mary is a creature like others means that her sinlessness reveals the possibility of complete redemption for created beings in general, and is thus a sign of hope to all. Karl Rahner has argued that, more than this, Mary's immaculate conception directs our attention to the goodness that already pervades the creation.[3] For whatever wickedness there is in the world – and we all see or hear of enough examples of evil that we should need no convincing of its vast extent – it remains the case that God's creation is a work of grace, and that the fact that anything is held in existence at all is evidence of God's continuing goodness at the foundation of all things. In Mary, whose vocation was to be the bearer of consummate goodness, that righteousness was never tarnished. But in all other people, and in the rest of creation, the grace that shines out in her draws our attention to the same grace as it works throughout the cosmos.

When God makes the new creation in Christ from his mother Mary, he does this by returning to the foundations of the universe, to the pure, untarnished Chaos that comes immediately from his own being, as the stuff out of which the new creation will arise. And Mary as Chaos, as creation's righteous beginning, is Mary in whom there has never been sin.

That the Immaculate Conception is of cosmic significance is represented in the painting by Velázquez. It shows Mary as the Woman of the Apocalypse, described in chapter twelve of the book of the Apocalypse, or Revelation. The book takes its name from the claim that its contents were given as a special revelation to St John the Divine on the island of Patmos, and the painting that Velázquez made to accompany *The Immaculate Conception* shows St John having the vision of the woman. The Apocalypse is concerned with the last times – with the end of the world and the last judgement – and the woman, who is a figure for the Church, but who has also been commonly identified with Mary, is 'clothed with the sun, with a crown of twelve stars, and with the moon beneath her feet'. She is in labour and gives birth to a male child. A dragon tries to eat the child, who is whisked up to heaven, and the mother is taken to a place of safety in the desert. This image was used to represent the immaculate conception because it is concerned with the final defeat of evil at the end of time: the child is Christ, and the dragon, who is Satan, Christ's enemy and the perpetrator of all evil is eventually cast down. Mary's sinless conception is emblematic of Christ's victory over Satan, since she is the first person in whom the Devil had no part, and the woman of the Apocalypse stands for the completion of the work of redemption that we see both begun and incipiently fulfilled in Christ's mother.

Yet the painting is concerned not only with the end times, but also with the beginning. For the woman depicted in it is also the figure of Wisdom, present with God before the foundation of the world, participating in the work of creation. As she is the Blessed Virgin, she is conceived in the mind

Figure 8. Diego Velázquez: *The Immaculate Conception* (detail),
National Gallery, London

of God from all eternity to be the mother of the incarnate Word, and her
conception in time is the earthly realization of a mystery prepared from
the womb before the dawn of the world.

Some of the emblems in the painting are taken from the Song of Songs,
and represent both Mary's miraculous virginity and her sinlessness. The
fountain, for example, is the 'sealed fountain', which signifies that her
virginity was unbroken and that her moral integrity was likewise unim-
paired. However, there is one element of the painting that is visually less
pronounced than the others, and whose symbolic meaning is also less
immediately obvious. This is a ship, which can be seen through the
translucent moon (Figure 8).

The Virgin Mary has long been associated with the sea. Sometimes she
is the protectress of seafarers for whom the sea is dangerous and unpredictable. It is in this capacity that she bears the title *Stella Maris*, or 'Star
of the Sea'. She is the lodestar who guides those who travel on the turbulent
seas of mortal life safely into the port of heaven. Sometimes she herself
travels by boat, as did Our Lady of Boulogne when, during the seventh
century, she arrived at the Gualish port, accompanied by angels, in a boat
with neither sail nor oars (Figure 2). In learned writing, Mary is 'the ship
of the merchant, who brings her food from afar' (Proverbs 31.14), which is
to say, she is the vessel who bears God incarnate, the eucharistic bread of

life, to the faithful.[4] And, as we have already seen, she is the deep from the beginning of creation.

Water is a natural symbol for prime matter. Water takes the shape of any vessel into which it is poured, and water removed from water makes little difference to the appearance of the water that remains. Yet the sea is more dynamic than this, and has often been a symbol for Chaos – both for Chaos as evil and Chaos as the primal state out of which the world was made. The sea may be the dwelling-place of monsters such as Leviathan. In the Babylonian epic of Marduk, the world is created out of the body of a sea monster, Tiamat. It is for this reason that, in the book of the Apocalypse, the account of the culmination of the victory of good and the establishment of God's reign includes the observation, 'and the sea was no more' (Apocalypse 21.1). Yet, perhaps because the Christian culture of the West has evolved amongst nations of hearty seafarers, or perhaps because we have perceived something that was missed by the visionary of the Apocalypse, we have had little space for the symbol of a sea-less universe. And significantly, when Velásquez brings together the beginning and the end, in an image of creation perfected, he includes the primal waters.

Notes

1 A brief account of the history of the doctrine is given in Boss, S.J., *Empress and Handmaid: On Nature and Gender in the Cult of the Virgin Mary*, Cassell, 2000, London, 123–55.

2 Lulio, R., *Libro de la Concepcion Virginal* [Latin text with Spanish trans. A. de Zepeda], Baltazar Vivien, Brussels, 1664.

3 Rahner, K., 'The Immaculate Conception', in *Theological Investigations*, Vol. 1 (trans. C. Ernst), Darton, Longman & Todd, London, 1974, 201–13. A simple exposition of this is given in Endean, P., 'How to think about Mary's privileges', in *Priests and People* 7.5, May 2003, 190–5, at 193.

4 D'Arcy, A.M., *Wisdom and the Grail: The Image of the Vessel in the 'Queste Del Saint Graal' and Malory's 'Tale of Sankgreal'*, Four Courts Press, Dublin, 2000, 295.

Index